RECIPES
from a
SPANISH
VILLAGE

RECIPES
from a
SPANISH
VILLAGE

PEPITA ARIS

Special photography by
Linda Burgess

CONRAN OCTOPUS

For my mother, who gave me my name and
bought a house in Spain

First published in 1990 by
Conran Octopus Limited
37 Shelton Street
London WC2H 9HN

Both metric and imperial quantities are
given in the recipes. Use either all metric or
all imperial, as the two are not interchangeable.

Project Editor: Cortina Butler
Art Director: Mary Evans
Edited by: Denise Bates
Designer: Christine Wood
Picture Research: Nadine Bazar
Production: Julia Golding
Home Economist: Jane Suthering
Assisted by: Meg Jansz
Photographic Stylist: Debbie Patterson
Painted Pottery: Barbara Mullarney Wright
Line Artwork: Conny Jude

British Library Cataloguing in Publication Data
Aris, Pepita
Recipes from a Spanish village.
1. Food: Spanish dishes
I. Title
641.5946

ISBN 1-85029-270-1

Typeset by Elite Typesetting Techniques, Southampton
Printed in Hong Kong

CONTENTS

INTRODUCTION

9

INSIDE A SPANISH STORECUPBOARD

10

TAPAS AND SOUPS

19

EGGS, RICE AND PASTA

41

VEGETABLES AND SALADS

61

FISH AND SHELLFISH

81

MEAT, POULTRY AND GAME

99

DESSERTS AND DRINKS

123

INDEX AND ACKNOWLEDGMENTS

140

INTRODUCTION

SPANISH FOOD EMBRACES A WORLD of sun and colour. It has the immediacy of food picked only when it is ripe, or cooked and eaten almost directly from the sea. It is honest food, bringing a few local products together to make a dish. And it is, above all, simple food, but cooked carefully, with an understanding of the very best way to exploit what it offers.

Spain is an unexplored territory for most cooks, who may have no more than a casual holiday aquaintance from visits to the beaches of the south. But the world of Spanish villages is unknown, and your kitchen shelf is unlikely to contain a book on Spanish fish cookery, or the cookery of any particular region of Spain. Unlike the food of Italy and France, for instance, Spanish food, with a couple of famous exceptions, is undiscovered even within Europe.

This is real food, village food – direct, simple and tasty. The recipes are suggested by the flavours, textures and colours of the ingredients themselves, and are not distorted by decoration or artifice in any way. Their secret lies in years of direct experience, experience which has shown that certain things combine in a particularly successful way. *No se admiten trampas en la cocina*, the Spaniards would say – no tricks to disguise indifferent food in the kitchen.

Occasionally the ingredients for some of these recipes may require a little hunting down. But while a few Spanish recipes take time, it is fortunately not *your* time. The dishes are quickly prepared and you can then sit back and wait while they cook: there is little fussing around. Spanish dishes also fall into a natural rhythm. One dish may leave you with exactly the ingredient needed – such as cooked chickpeas, or boiled bacon – to complete the next one in Spanish style. The Spaniards also like single things on a plate. This is a relief from the tyranny of having to make lots of dishes for each main course, while a sequence of salads and other dishes is also easier to serve.

The length of some recipes does not mean they are difficult. They may often be quicker to cook than to explain, and readers familiar with foods like artichokes, or salt cod, can skip through the explanations, which I have offered for those who are meeting these foods for the first time.

Certain things are impossible to make well here without the native fish, shellfish and sometimes vegetables, and every cook worth his or her salt makes a contribution to the recipe cooked. But I do like recipes to respect their origins, and not to get away from what they are – a picnic dish to eat in the fields, a fisherman's stew, a Sunday pot containing the best the farmyard has on offer. I don't like them sieved, decorated and the like, with no respect for the origin or nature of the dish.

I have a prejudice in favour of the natural, original way of cooking traditional things too – but speeded along by using modern machinery. I have tried here to present the old tastes, refined perhaps, but not disguised or obliterated by modern ideas of what tastes good. Some recipes – very few – have been slightly rethought to make them lighter or healthier, but they are not repackaged for the international market.

Spanish cooking is largely regional cooking, based on the produce of an immediate area. Though I have had a house in one of the prettiest villages of Andalusia for nearly twenty years, these recipes come from all over a country that varies quite markedly. Many generalizations have been made about Spain, the famous one being that the cooking is like the climate: 'In the north they stew, on the plains they roast and in the south they fry.' Different provinces, too, are known for their different talents. The Basques are knowledgeable cooks, the Catalans experimental and adventurous, their cooking is progressive and dazzling, with a capacity to take you by surprise just when you thought you knew it. But all over Spain you will find colour on a plate and common sense about the food that is available turned into an art.

I can do no more than Richard Ford, the 19th-century traveller, and 'skim the subject, which is indeed fat and unctuous'. I hope you will go to Spain and seek out its traditional recipes there. Meanwhile, experience some of its pleasures by cooking them yourself.

PEPITA ARIS

INSIDE A SPANISH STORECUPBOARD

AGUARDIENTE

'Toothwater' it is not, though that is how Richard Ford referred to it, some 130 years ago. It is usually a colourless *eau-de-vie*, the anis-flavoured kind being popular for cooking, but the term includes any distilled liquor. *Aguardiente de orujo* is a grape brandy, like *marc*, made from skins and pips.

ALMONDS AND HAZELNUTS

Almendras were introduced by the Moors, and almonds are basic to most biscuits and many Spanish sauces. Toasted almonds and hazelnuts, *avellanas*, are exquisite and partner sherry well. Toast them in a low oven at about 150° C (300° F, gas 2) for 20 minutes to bring out their flavour.

ARTICHOKES

Alcachofas are served whole or the bases only may be prepared (mainly for salads). Hearts (whole immature artichokes) and bases are both sold canned. To prepare the base see page 103, to cook and eat whole see page 74.

BACALAO

Cod is not a Mediterranean fish, but the Spaniards immediately took to salted, dried cod. The phrase *cortar el bacalao*, 'first choice at the *bacalao*', means to be 'top dog'. Indispensable as a Lenten food, and associated with Good Friday, it has become a year-round favourite, though it looks stiff and rather unappealing when raw.

Bacalao increases in weight by half when soaked, but this is lost again in discarded bones and skin. Soak the fish for 24 hours – longer if it is not to be cooked in any liquid – preferably under running water, otherwise change the water 2–3 times. Remove all skin, bones, fins and badly discoloured flesh. The thick centre cuts are prized most highly, and should not taste salty after proper preparation.

BEANS

Alubias, in a wide selection of colours, are dried beans and each area of Spain has its own local favourite. Introduced from America in the 16th century, these beans alleviated what was at that time a tedious diet, based on broad beans, *habas*, and chickpeas. The nearest bean to *faba*, the white bean of Galicia, is the butter bean. All dried beans have a natural affinity with salted meat.

Fresh beans are also eaten, of course: *pochas* are podded fresh haricot beans, and fresh green beans are *judías verdes*.

Soak dried beans overnight in cold water, or for 1 hour in boiling water. They more than double in weight after cooking. Modern varieties, however, do not need the long cooking of traditional recipes, and can break up disagreeably. Fresh and soaked kidney beans will both cook in around 1 hour.

BRANDY

Coñac is cheap in Spain and is used as the French might use Martini, to bolster wine sauces. The big seller is the inappropriately named Soberano, which is less sweet. But the fashion is increasingly for sweeter, caramelized after-dinner brandies: like Veterano, whose cut-out bull advertisements so contribute to the southern skyline of Spain, and Magno, which is smooth and aromatic.

BREAD

Spanish bread is white and of excellent quality, freshly baked every day, and sold first thing in the morning as rolls, under names like *bollo* or *chica*, 'little girl', and later in the day as the larger *pan*. Wholemeal bread, and some rye or cornmeal, can be found in the north-west corner of the country.

Bread is the standard accompaniment to food, in a country where few dishes are paired. Bread is also eaten as a *bocadillo*, a crusty roll sandwich, with olive oil replacing butter. The *cocas* of Mallorca are the nearest thing to an Italian pizza.

Stale bread is used as a thickener for sauces, for it will hold a little fat in suspension; the result is light and not greasy. *Torrijas* are a children's sweet: stale bread dipped in milk, then egg-coated, fried and sugared.

BUTIFARRA

A common white sausage in Catalonia and Mallorca, it is made of pork, tripe and pine-nuts and spiced with cinnamon and cumin. It is good grilled. There are also black *butifarrones* – a nickname for the middle classes in their black coats.

CARDOON

The *cardo* is popular in Navarre, a relative of the globe artichoke but less well known. The stalks are boiled and eaten with butter or béchamel sauce.

CHARD

Acelga is an old vegetable round the Mediterranean. The glossy dark leaves and bright-white stalks can be eaten together, but are most often separated. Spinach can be substituted for the leaves of chard.

CHEESE

Mountains and cheese go together, and ewes' milk cheeses are found all over Europe's most mountainous country. Goats' milk cheeses are made in both the south and north, but only in the wetter north can one find cheese from cows' milk. Most cheeses are still unpasteurized.

The most famous cheese, and the only one exported in any quantity, is Manchego. It is best known in a black rind. Spanish cheeses vary more widely in the course of ageing than the cheddars we know, and Manchego may be mild and quite soft, or strong and hard. Because it is made of ewes' milk it is expensive – more so than Parmesan, which makes the best substitute. Manchego-style cheeses stored in olive oil are a good buy, as they age without drying.

The most famous blue cheese is Cabrales, and the similar Picón, from the Picos de Europa where it is made. Creamy, blue-veined and sold wrapped in leaves, it is the Spanish Roquefort: a gourmet treat.

Fresh cheeses are made round the country, like *queso de Burgos*, widely available in Spain and eaten as a dessert with honey. From Galicia the creamy

SAVIA DE LA VIDA ES EL ZUMO DE LA FRUTA DE ESPAÑA

Bevorzugt SPANIENS Edelobst.
Demandez partout les Fruits d'ESPAGNE.
Eat more SPANISH fruits.

tetilla is famous for the name 'titty', and its gentle breast shape.

Smoked cheeses include one from Roncal, with tiny holes, and the shiny, amber-coloured San Simón, which looks like a ripe pear.

Soft cheeses are eaten with fruit or honey as a dessert, but firm and hard ones are most popular plain, with bread, at either end of a meal. Cooking with cheese is not a Spanish habit, though the spread of Italian pasta dishes in the 19th century introduced cheese sauces. Cheese is grated over baked vegetables like aubergines and egged-and-crumbed fried cheese, *queso frito*, is a popular *tapa*.

CHICKPEAS

These *garbanzos* are 'the potato of the land', commented Richard Ford. They are sold dried or *en remojo*, soaked, are eaten everywhere, and are honoured in Madrid with names like *gabrieles*,

angels, and *trompitos*, trumpets.

They are also sold ready-cooked and salted, particularly during festivals, as a *tapa* and for giving to children.

Soak overnight in three times their volume of cold water, or in boiling water for 1 hour. I find modern varieties cook in an hour, but they are one of the few pulses that do not spoil if overcooked and are intact after $2\frac{1}{2}$ hours. They reheat well.

CHILLIES

Spanish cooking is distinguished by its subtle use of capsicums. The smallest and hottest is *guindilla*, lending heat to the dishes of the north-west. A little cayenne pepper is a simple substitute.

A sweet chilli that is not hot is an unfamiliar idea, but the *choricero* has had great influence on Spanish cooking. You can see it drying in red bunches, hung from every balcony in villages like Laguardia in Rioja, during the autumn. It gives their name, plus colour and piquancy, to *chorizo* sausages, and is an essential ingredient of Basque dishes *a la vizcaina*. Another sweet chilli is the *ñora*, called *romesco* in Catalonia (see page 88).

CHORIZO

Chorizos are sausages containing paprika from the *choricero* pepper. There are two main types.

Cured *chorizos* are the larger, about 5 cm (2 in) in diameter and are sliced and eaten raw on bread as a *tapa*. Best known are those from Rioja, and from Pamplona. They are fine-flavoured but chewy, though the Pamplona *chorizo* is more finely textured. A few are exported from Spain but a big factory in Belgium produces them for consumption in northern Europe.

Cooking *chorizos* are a local affair and

may be smoked or fresh, but will always be fatty. 'A little capsicum-red fellow ... with some garlic-juice – not a flood, but a flavouring breath', this is *the* scarlet sausage and the heavy paprika content leaches out in cooking, to colour potatoes or soups red. *Chorizos* linked by scarlet string will be far hotter than others with plain string.

Cooking *chorizos* are made all over the country, but those from Extremadura and Asturias are most famous. For *cocido madrileño* (see page 104), the first choice is *chorizo* from Cantimpalos in Segovia. *Chistorra* is a thin red sausage from Navarre which looks like *chorizo*.

Italian delicatessens are the best place to find paprika sausages. For frying, fresh garlic sausages make acceptable substitutes, but for boiling, look for smoked sausages. There are also supermarkets imitations, adequate but not as good as the real thing, and smoked sausages from Eastern Europe like *kabanos*.

CIDER

Cider apples may have originated on the Black Sea, but the Basques feel they perfected the drink. It is strongly alcoholic and in the *sidrería* shops you can drink all the cider you wish, for a small fee, and eat in the intervals. Cider is made in wet Asturias, too, and here it replaces wine.

CINNAMON

The association of cinnamon with lamb and poultry dates from Moorish times – originally for its antiseptic properties. Now *canela* is much used for all Spanish sweets, including their favourite biscuits and ice creams. Cinnamon is partnered with chocolate, rather than vanilla, for the Spaniards

missed the Mexican association of these two altogether.

FAT

Though the Spaniards are Mediterranean, and have always liked olive oil, they adopted lard, *saim*, or pig's fat under the influence of northern barbarians. Because it made the food richer, pork fat has become synonymous with abundance. Butter is used in Galicia and the Pyrenees, but it is not traditional elsewhere.

The combination of olive oil and fat is a very basic one in Spanish cooking. Pork fat, incidentally, has half the cholesterol of butter. TOCINO, sold as blocks of hard fat, and soft *manteca de cerdo*, encased in a plastic sausage, are both used for frying. *Manteca colorada* (see page 28), fat coloured with paprika (but not necessarily with added meat) is typical of Seville and Cordoba. It is used for frying and is also spread on toast for breakfast.

A by-product of pork fat is crackling. Called *chicharro*, this is sold as a snack at corner stores.

I find the easiest non-vegetable fat, and the best for flavour, is rendered fat from poultry. Cornfed chickens give off a considerable amount (of vegetable origin, but tasting of poultry), while duck fat keeps well.

GARLIC

Garlic is fundamental to Spanish cooking, although wrongly thought to dominate it. Its importance is illustrated by the phrase *estar en el ajo* 'in the garlic', meaning to be 'in the know'. Used raw or cooked, garlic has two quite different flavours, the first pungent, the second suggestive. A dish *al ajillo* is flavoured with chopped garlic, while *ajo* means whole cloves appear,

and they may be eaten like white beans, made mild by long cooking.

Few books bother to explain that when garlic is the first ingredient into the frying pan, it is there only to flavour the oil, and is automatically discarded. It otherwise turns to 'tea leaves'.

Garlic is an essential part of *sofrito*, that sequence of soft onion, with garlic and chopped parsley added, that is at the base of so many Spanish rice dishes and sauces. It is also part of a *picada*, a thickening mixture for a sauce, added at the end. Its most famous use, though, is in *alioli* (see pages 54 and 101). The original sauce, which dates back to Roman times in Spain, was just garlic in oil, used as a condiment. Nowadays it is frequently made with egg yolks and served with grilled meat and fried fish, or added to soups on serving.

HAM AND CURED MEATS

Spanish raw ham is very famous (see JAMÓN), but cooked ham and bacon are also sold. Small quantities of ham are frequently needed in Spanish cooking and I prefer this cut from a raw smoked corner gammon or knuckle. The latter is a small, cheap supermarket joint, with a useful bone for Spanish-style recipes. It can be split into two or three pieces, which can then be frozen. Gammon and bacon chops are easy to buy and, being thicker than bacon, cube neatly. Melt the fat scraps for frying.

In Spain various types of cured pork are on sale. The famous *lacón* of Galicia is the cured front leg of the pig, (our gammon knuckle), and salted ears, tails and trotter are all appreciated for the flavour they give to stews.

There are also *salones*: cured meat from lamb, kid and beef. The best known of these is *cecina*, salted, air-dried beef, called 'bull's ham'.

JAMÓN SERRANO

A gourmet feast by itself, this raw ham is much in demand. It has a beautiful chewy texture served in thin slices on bread, and is also used for cooking. Traditionally *serrano* is carved with the grain, along, rather than into, the ham but less finely than Italian *prosciutto*, which is the nearest substitute.

The most famous hams are cured where there are winter snows, hence their name of 'mountain' hams. Jabugo in Huelva and Trevélez in Granada are famous in the south, though the Duc de St Simon, in the 19th century, thought the hams of Montánchez in Extremadura were the most exquisite thing he had tasted, and hams from Lérida and Teruel, both in the east, are also well known.

The best *jamón serrano* comes from the black or red Iberian pig, which roams half-wild in the mountains, eating acorns, which marbles the flesh with flavourful fat. Lesser raw hams, from white pigs, are much leaner and so are widely eaten.

The pigs are slaughtered in autumn, and the hams packed in salt for 8–10 days, then hung in airy rooms upstairs for the 6 winter months. When the weather turns warm, the hams begin to sweat salt, which is allowed to happen for one week. They are then moved to cool cellars and hung there for the 6 warm months.

Jamón is also used for cooking, as it has to be trimmed every now and then for slicing. Old bones, called *añejos*, are sold for boiling.

LOMO EMBUCHADO

A smoked, pink, pig's loin cured whole in a sausage casing, it tastes like good ham. Sliced into neat rounds, it is a delicious, but expensive, form of cold meat, eaten on bread as a *tapa*.

LONGANIZA

A thin, hard, bland sausage, like a somewhat fatty salami inside, *longaniza* hangs in a wonderful hank round and round its own wooden bar. It is used for cooking, and the word may cover other varieties of sausage.

MORCILLA

A black sausage, in links or occasionally rings, it is dark both because it contains pig's blood and because it is smoked. This, and the unusually large amount of onion in it, give it a rich flavour. It may also contain pine-nuts, rice and cinnamon.

The most famous *morcillas* come from Extremadura and Asturias, where they are a principal ingredient of *fabada* (see page 106). They are always cooked. The best substitutes to use are Scottish black puddings and those from Lancashire.

There is a second type, called *morcilla dulce*, which can be eaten as a *tapa*. The spicy sweetness and dark colour, with a rich, tongue-clinging creamy fat, make it the nearest thing to eating Christmas pudding with cream.

MUSHROOMS

Champiñones, from the French, are cultivated mushrooms, but the Spaniards prefer *setas*, wild ones, and *hongos*, a smaller category of fungus. From April, when the mild *moixernons* first appear, to the end of the autumn, mushroom picking is a national hobby. *Boletos*, ceps, and *rossinyols*, chanterelles, are the most popular. Best-known and, dare I say, slightly over-rated, are *rovellons* (see page 66). Wild mushrooms are usually cooked simply, or added to game casseroles, and all have local names.

OIL

Spanish olive oil is usually 'pure' – a mixture of virgin and refined oils. With its modest olive taste and comparatively high acidity, it is better for mayonnaise than higher-priced and more famous virgin oils. In the 1970s much was exported to Italy – and re-labelled. Since the Arabs promoted its use in the kitchen, it has been used for frying and makes a surprisingly light and attractive sauce in liaison with a liquid. It is the healthiest of fats and also the safest for deep frying.

Spanish virgin oil is easier to buy abroad than it is in Spain. The best is made at Baena, near Jaén, and around Lérida at Borjas Blancas, the Sierra de Segura and Siurana. It is very fruity – some taste almost appley.

Sunflowers, cut early when black, are also pressed to make a cheaper cooking oil, *aciete de girasol*.

ONION

Cebollas must be fried very slowly, to bring out their sweetness, quite different from their raw taste. Bigger than an orange, the yellow Spanish onion is the sweetest and mildest of all. A *sofrito* of slowly-fried onion, with garlic, then tomato, added, is basic to many rice and soup recipes.

The oversize spring onions, called *calçots* in Catalan and *cebollones* in Spanish, are good grilled (see page 65).

PACHARÁN

Spain's most popular generic liqueur, this dark, sweet anis-flavoured drink is made from sloes. It is drunk 'on the rocks' and also makes a good fish sauce. Zoco is the best-known brand.

PAPRIKA AND CAYENNE PEPPER

Pimentón fuerte, hot pepper, is cayenne, while *pimentón dulce* – called coloured pepper, *pimentón colorado*, in the south – is paprika.

Paprika is an extremely important spice in the Spanish kitchen, used before frying, rather than as a cosmetic touch at the end. A little paprika will also help the balance of a dish, in the absence of traditional Spanish varieties of vegetable peppers, and eke out the more expensive saffron.

PEPPERS

Spain has two types of pepper, only one of which is exported. The finest pepper in Spain is the *pimiento piquillo*, which is long and pointed: it means 'beak-shaped'. It is chiefly grown in Navarre and Rioja and it is distinctly hot. In Spain it's these thin-skinned peppers that are stuffed with salt cod or minced meat, made easier by their being sold ready in jars.

The fleshy, bell-shaped pepper, called *morrón*, 'knobbly' pepper, in Spain, is extremely popular, though it is worth remembering that the green pepper is actually an underripe pepper of another colour. Red peppers will always be sweeter and contain more vitamins. In Spain these are usually grilled or baked to remove the skin, after which the flesh may disintegrate to a sweet juice and a beautiful purée. These have a better flavour than canned red *pimientos*, which are much used as a short cut, because they are sold already skinned.

PINE-NUTS

These tiny cream-coloured nuts are extracted from the cones of stone pines, and are consequently expensive. The flavour is astringent, yet rich, much liked for sauces, vegetable dishes and expensive little cakes like *piñonates*.

RICE

One of the glories of Spanish cooking, Spanish rice is between a round and medium grain, and its unique characteristic is to absorb liquid without any stickiness (which is induced into other rices). Italian *risotto* rice was introduced by the Arabs to Italy at the same time, and is similar, though cooked very differently. Risotto rice is stirred regularly to encourage the rice to become sticky, but *paella* rice is washed to remove starch, then cooked without being stirred.

The rice should absorb the exact amount of liquid in which it is cooked, leaving it flavoured, but each grain separate. Consequently, the quality of the stock is important. The rice will absorb double its own volume of liquid, or a little more, depending on the width of the pan, the heat source and the other ingredients. For four people allow 400 g (14 oz) rice and 900 ml (1½ pt) stock.

Indoors, cook rice over a heat diffuser, which spreads and diminishes the heat. Big pans are tricky: a thin or deep one is best cooked in the oven at 180° C (350°F, gas 4) after the last stir.

SAFFRON

Azafrán is an Arab spice, though it was introduced to Spain by the Romans, and Spain now produces the world's best saffron. In La Mancha the saffron crocuses flower overnight and are picked round Santa Teresa's day in mid-October. The enormous expense of the spice reflects the fact that its three pistils must be plucked by hand from every flower. Nevertheless it is not a spice to economize on. Indeed, Norman Douglas once said that, 'A man who is stingy with saffron is capable of seducing his own grandmother.'

A 2.5 g phial of Spanish saffron will include about 50 deep-red stamens, enough for an ordinary dish for 10 people or one dish *espléndido*. As the price of saffron has gone up, so the size of packets of saffron powder has gone down. They are now often 1 g, meaning 3 packets for a big dish. Cheap saffron, or from a doubtful source, may be a dye or made of safflower, *cártamo*.

I have burnt many expensive saffron strands trying to toast them on modern heat sources – they are just too hot! However papers of powder may be dry-fried until the paper colours. Before using, soak stamens for 20 minutes, and dissolve powder in 2 tablespoons of hot liquid.

SALCHICHÓN

A Spanish salami, smooth and pink with specks of chopped fat and whole white peppercorns but no paprika, it makes a good *tapa* and stores well.

SALT AND PEPPER

The simpler the recipe, the more important is intelligent seasoning. Spain has good coarse salt, while that from Cadiz contains some saltpetre, which is good for hams and preserved sausages. The Catalans are generous users of black pepper, *pimienta*.

SHERRY

A mispronunciation of Jerez, sherry is a fortified wine from the south-west. In Spain dry sherry accompanies fish and *tapas*, but sherry's high alcohol content has made it on the whole a before- or after-dinner wine.

Sherries are blended in a *solera* system of stacked barrels, where new wine goes in the top and wine is then moved down to fill the lower tiers and drawn from the bottom. They are ranked for export in different sweetnesses, though in Spain each of them can vary quite widely within a given category. *Fino* is pale gold, crisp and dry, and *manzanilla* is the most delicate type of *fino*, influenced by the sea air of Sanlúcar, where it is stored. *Amontillado* is fuller-bodied, more golden and nuttier, and conventionally medium dry. *Palo cortado* comes in sweetness between this and *oloroso*, a mature, and usually sweeter, sherry.

The neighbouring district of Montilla-Moriles produces very similar sherry-type wines which achieve the same alcoholic strengths without forti-fication though some are, in fact, fortified. The pale dry Montilla is best known.

SOBRASADA

A soft, pâté-like sausage, largely of pork fat with some raw cured pork, it is flavoured and coloured with paprika. It may be served in pots for spreading on bread or slices may go on top of large *ensaimada* breads. It is eaten in Mallorca and Catalonia.

SQUID AND CUTTLEFISH

When freshly caught their skins are pink, greying out of the water. Squid are mainly fried, or used in rice dishes or salads, but smaller ones, called *chipirones*, are stuffed.

Cuttlefish, called *jibia* or *sepia* – and *choco* if tiny – are stuffed or stewed. They are prized for the black ink, in a bag inside them that makes cleaning all of them a little tricky.

STOCK

People curl up at the edges at the men-tion of fish stock. All I can say is: don't. First, it is very quick – unlike other stocks – taking 30 minutes at the out-side. Second, the ingredients are not so difficult: look at prawn stock on page 59, for example. All it needs is prawn heads and Martini.

The ingredients for the real thing – fish skin, bones and heads can be bought in many street markets and supermarkets where fresh fish is sold. Get the messy work done for you by the fishmonger, but take the bits away with you. Then simmer with an onion, celery stalk, bay leaves, parsley stalks and wine. Strain and add a strip of lemon zest to the hot stock.

Some supermarkets carry reduced fish stock and good fish soups. Canned clam juice and products like Clamato can also be used, while the Swiss make passable fish stock cubes.

If using cubes, remember two things. They should be used under-strength with something else like vegetable water: a quarter of the quan-tity in wine is also a good rule. And never, never use a cube and then reduce it. This will only expose the artificial base. Instead, look at the final amount of liquid and calculate the appropriate portion of cube.

Chicken stocks can be made with carcasses without legs, from butchers who sell breasts off the bone, and from chicken wings, and in Spain it is tra-ditional to include a ham bone, which can be used several times. To remove any fat, draw strips of kitchen paper over the surface of the liquid.

TOCINO

Salted pork fat, but from the belly not the back, *tocino* sometimes has rib bones in it. It is in a block, cut to order. Rendered cubes of *tocino* are wonderful for frying onions.

Tocino is much more fatty than salt-cured pork belly and recipes have been adjusted for this. The word is some-times used for bacon.

TOMATOES

Really ripe tomatoes are used for sauce in Spain, lesser ones being relegated to salad. Ripe tomatoes are easy to peel: others may need 10 seconds in boiling water first. The flesh is then neatly cubed for salad, and dissolves easily to make a sauce. Add the leftover skin and seeds to stock, where they attract grease and scum, helping the stock to strain cleanly.

Outside Spain, canned tomatoes are often a redder, riper choice than fresh ones. A quick sauce is made from canned tomatoes added to *sofrito* (see ONION), then reduced and seasoned.

VINEGAR

Wine vinegar is used for vinaigrette and sauces. The vineyards of the south make sherry vinegar from young sher-ries that are reserved because of their high acidity. These are matured in wood and concentrated, so they are more intense than most wine vinegars.

WINE

Out to lunch on a special occasion, a Spanish family would probably choose a wine from either Rioja or Penedès, the two areas which took in French winemakers, when the vineyards of the French were destroyed by phylloxera in the 19th century.

There is no longer a natural connec-tion between regional food and wines in many areas, although Spain has more vineyards than any other coun-try. Starting in the 19th century, and at an ever faster pace since the 1970s, the wines have been rethought with a ruth-less commercial logic.

Spanish wines are blended wines. There are no restrictions on where the winemaker buys his grapes, or on the proportions in which he combines several types. The weather is hot and varies less than in other parts of Europe, too. So Spanish wines are sold on the winemakers' skill and the name on the bottle is like a brand name.

The white wines are unusually diverse. First there are those with a 'sherry taste': dry, golden and very high in alcohol, like the white of Extre-madura, the Chiclana of Cadiz and dry

Montillas. Then there are the aristo-cratic, oak-aged whites, like Marqués de Murrieta, which have the virtues of their red counterparts. Rueda, home to the white Marqués de Riscal, makes a fruity white from traditional grapes.

But many whites were thought to be insufficiently fruity or crisp and now wines are made in the French style, both in Penedès, where they are out-standing, and in Rioja. Fresh and fruity, wines like Rioja's Monopole are popular in Spain as well as in the export market for which they were designed. The main thing against them is that the taste often fades more quickly than in the French models.

There is also a small class of fresh 'green' wines: the *alberiños* of Galicia, and white *chacolí* of which the Basques are so fond. *Cavas*, champagne-method sparklers, are popular and fine dessert wines are made from muscat grapes.

The young red wines make remark-ably pleasant, easy drinking, being fresh and very fruity. Spaniards mostly drink *vino corriente*, which is labelled with the *cosecha*, harvest year, and is one or two years old. They are considerably less fussy about matching wine and food than other nations whose best wine is more highly esteemed.

The two main wine lakes come from La Mancha and the Levante coast, the latter producing undistinguished, high-alcohol reds. At the other end of the scale is Ribero del Duero, which produces Spain's undisputed best red, the almost-unobtainable Vega de Sicilia. In between, a number of drink-able reds come from places like Toro and Valdepeñas, while many Navarre wines have the virtues of the better-known Rioja.

Rioja is Spain's best-known wine district, for it makes more complex wines that age well. Even so, less than half of its wine is wood-aged. The hallmark of Rioja is the whiff of vanilla that storage in oak casks gives to wine. New oak barrels make a wine taste strongly of vanilla. As the barrels are very expensive to replace, the winemakers move the wines around from barrel to barrel, sometimes four times in a year, to juggle each blend to best advantage. Minimum periods in the barrel are laid down for each class of wine. All white wines and *rosados*, rosés, must spend a minimum of 6 months in the barrel, while red wines must have a year, and *Gran reservas* a two-year minimum. For the remaining time they mature in the bottle.

Think of the better barrel-aged wines like racehorses in three classes: 3-year-olds, 4-year-olds and 6-year-olds. The first are *crianzas*, the second *reservas*, the last *Gran reservas*. Simple maths will tell you if a bottle is old for its class, and so may well have had longer in the barrel than the minimum laid down. *Gran reservas* are wines spot-ted for their potential and given pre-ferential treatment.

Some old-fashioned houses like Marqués de Murrieta and Muga go for longer barrel-ageing as part of their house style. Other modern *bodegas* like Faustino Martínez and Olarra favour the minimum amount of oak and age in the bottle instead, a style that is popular in America.

Penedès is the other area of Spain known for large-scale production of quality wines. These differ from Rioja in two ways. Very few are barrel-aged. They are modelled on French wines and Torres, in particular, produces a drier style of red than Rioja, which often includes French grapes, like Cabernet Sauvignon. The whites are fresh and fruity, using grapes like Chardonnay, and are more successful than attempts to do likewise in other parts of Spain. Also in the north-east, Raimat in Lérida produces successful wines from Cabernet Sauvignon.

TAPAS AND SOUPS

Tapas are a way of life in Spain, with drinks or as a starter. The rich array of soups — from chilled summer refreshers to hearty winter warmers — illustrates the geographical diversity of the country.

Left to right, from top PINCHITOS MORUNOS *(p 21)*, CHAMPIÑONES RELLENOS *(p 23)*, BUÑUELOS DE QUESO *(p 24)*, PELOTAS EN SALSA ROJA *(p 21)*, GAMBAS EN GABARDINAS *(p 26)*, MEJILLONES CON PIMIENTO VERDE Y ROJO *(p 26)*.

I CAN THINK OF NO PLACE where you can get such an extraordinary range of things to eat as in a *tapas* bar. The place promises drink and company, but the food is the lure to make you stay. Just as a Dubliner might go in search of ambiance and whiskeys, so a Spaniard *va de pinchos*, goes looking for *pinchos*, delicious titbits on skewers. A glorious selection is laid out on the bar, for the casual visitor to see, and to persuade him to linger.

The word *tapa* was originally used to mean a 'cover', a piece of bread, balanced over a drink in a hostelry to keep out the flies in hot weather. Sausage or cheese would then be perched on top to make the bread appealing and, in days gone by, these were included in the price of the drink.

To lure and tempt you, a whole range of flavours is offered in tiny portions, from the sophisticated and exotic to the bland and soothing. Tasting and sharing them becomes a communal activity. The simplest *tapas* include some of Spain's best ready-to-eat food: scarlet raw *serrano* ham, black-waxed Manchego cheese, chunks of spicy *chorizo* sausage and, above all, marinated olives: *aceitunas aliñadas*. From the king-sized Obregóns, almost as plump as walnuts, conventional green *sevillanas extras*, to the small green *manzanillas* and the tiny greyish-brown *arbequines*, no bigger than fat Malaga raisins, everyone has a favourite. There are black ones, too, *negra dulce perlas*, or oily *aragonésas*.

There are also warming dishes on offer, of the best-loved nursery foods, for is this not a place of consolation, where men go after the trials of work? Simple, direct flavours can be savoured in golden egg *tortilla*, *patatas bravas* – potatoes in a chilli-hot tomato sauce – or chicken in garlic, and there is soothing food in familiar sauces, like kidneys with sherry and a variety of meatballs in tomato sauce.

In *tapas* bars the Spaniards can indulge their passion for seafood. There, prawns are always on offer, then clams or mussels in white wine, marinated anchovies – and their backbones, fried to crunchy-crispness as a separate speciality – baby, stuffed squid, called *chipirones*, and the impenetrably dark potage of squid braised in its own ink.

Tapas will also be local dishes. In the Basque country you may find *angulas*, baby eels or elvers, of a gossamer thinness, tossed with hot chilli oil in an earthenware bowl. Small, fried *kokotxas*, which are hake cheeks, are another speciality, and *gambas en gabardinas*, prawns in a batter 'mackintosh', (see page 26) and pots of *txangurro*, or baked spider crab, may be found anywhere on the northern coast. Cadiz, in the south-west, is famous for its fried fish: like *acedías fritas*, baby soles, and *huevas*, crisp-fried fish roe. Shark, mostly dogfish, is appreciated stewed or battered. And, of course, there is the fried food that sums up Spain for the tourist, puffy rings of *calamares*, though in this corner of Spain squid are tiny ones, fried whole as *puntillitas*.

The idea behind *tapas* is that of a gap filler, an unwinder before the late dinner which is the habit in urban Spain. The food is also a prop for drinking, preventing one becoming drunk, and, in origin at least, largely a male affair.

Many *tapas* make a good starter to a meal. The Spaniards also appreciate a dish the more if it is an *entremés con apellido*, with a name or story attached to it. With these starters I have included soups, because of the way I thought the book would be used outside Spain. Spanish recipe books, however, group soups with one-pot meals and stews, and there is a very good reason for this. The pot of different meats, which are simmered together for the main course, also produces *caldo*, a beautiful broth, which is clear from very slow simmering. This is the basis of many soups, including the world-famous *consomé al Jerez*, which is more likely to be called *sopa viña A.B.* in Spain itself, from a sherry much favoured for it.

There are a few well-known cream soups, like the salt cod *puré de Vigilia*, eaten during Lent, and bread is the base for another class of thin soup. Mule drivers, obviously a spoiled lot, have a bread and red wine version called *sopa de loro*, while everyone knows the chilled garlic-scented *gazpacho*.

Each province has its fish soups, often laced with alcohol against bad sea-weather, like the mussel, tomato-and-*aguardiente sopa de mejillones* of the Catalans. The stew pot, full of fishy things, gives its name to another group, like the *caldeiradas* of Galicia (though in this book these fish soup-stews are included in Fish). In the countryside, however, the commonest of all soups are *potajes*: thick vegetable mixtures, full of this-and-that, like the cabbage-leaved *berzas*.

PELOTAS EN SALSA ROJA

TINY MEATBALLS
IN RED SHERRY SAUCE

There are quicker ways to make a tomato sauce, but this one is wonderfully simple. Its character depends on first-class pale dry *fino* sherry or Montilla wine.

SERVES 6–8

500 g (1 lb) minced pork or veal (or half and half)
100 g (4 oz) smoked raw gammon or bacon, minced
50 g (2 oz) stoned green olives, finely chopped
2 slices of stale bread
4 tablespoons lemon juice
finely grated zest of ½ lemon
¼ teaspoon coarse salt
pinch of cayenne pepper
2 small eggs, beaten, for coating
flour for coating
125–150 ml (4–5 fl oz) olive oil for frying

SALSA ROJA
1 onion, finely chopped
1 kg (2 lb) ripe tomatoes, without skin or seeds, or
800 g (1 lb 12 oz) canned tomatoes, with juice
2 tablespoons olive oil
200 ml (6 fl oz) good fino sherry or Montilla wine

Start with the sauce. Fry the onion very slowly in the olive oil, letting it soften and darken. Add the tomato and simmer, stirring occasionally with a spoon, until the sauce is much reduced. (It's quicker to do this in two pans.)

Soak the bread in the lemon juice, then squeeze out lightly. Combine with all the other ingredients for the meatballs – this is easy in a food processor. Roll into balls the size of large marbles, then roll them in beaten egg. Shake them in a plastic bag containing flour, or to and fro on a floured plate, until lightly coated.

Heat the oil and fry the meatballs in one or two pans, shaking the pan(s) to and fro every now and then, so they roll over and colour evenly. When they are cooked, stir the *fino* into the sauce, pour over the meatballs and bring back to the boil. Spear them with cocktail sticks to serve.

PINCHITOS MORUNOS

SMALL SPICY MOORISH KEBABS

In Andalusia every village store sells the spice mixture for these kebabs, in a little box decorated with a red-turbaned Moor with a white beard. It's probably Spain's only ready-made spice mixture. It was pointed out to me that six of the ten spices in *pinchitos* are also in curry powder, and so a mild curry powder makes an excellent base to start from.

In Morocco the dish is made with lamb, but in Spain it is usually of pork, which has the big advantage that it can be marinated with salt. The first *pinchitos* I ever ate were slim strips of pork about 5 cm (2 in) long, 'stitched' with a small wooden skewer of about twice the length: more interesting than cubes which, of course, taste the same. Strips can be cut from pork veined with fat – shoulder or spare rib – following the natural grain.

SERVES 10–12

500 g (1 lb) small pork cubes, or pork shoulder
steaks or spare rib chops, cut into strips
2 garlic cloves, finely chopped
2 teaspoons salt
1 teaspoon mild curry powder
1 teaspoon coriander seeds, ground
1 teaspoon paprika
¼ teaspoon dried thyme
plenty of freshly ground black pepper
3 tablespoons olive oil
1 tablespoon lemon juice

Crush the garlic with the salt in a mortar, or with the flat of a knife on a board, then moving the paste to a bowl. Work in all the other marinading ingredients. Skewer the pork and turn the pieces (2–2½ dozen) in the marinade in a shallow dish, making sure that every one is coated all round. Leave to marinate for 2 hours and preferably longer.

Heat the grill and cover the grid with foil. Spread the *pinchitos* out well and give them 2–3 minutes on each side, flipping them over with tongs.

21

POLLO AL AJILLO AL ESTILO DE PARELLADA

BONELESS GARLIC CHICKEN MORSELS

Chicken with garlic is one of the most typical Spanish dishes. It is generally the Spanish method to cut up birds with a chopper through the bone. This dish, however, is boneless, thanks to Juli Parellada, a 19th-century Barcelona dandy, who dared to ask for his *paella* 'with all bones removed'.

SERVES 6

1.1 kg (2½ lb) chicken, preferably free-range
4 fat garlic cloves, finely chopped
2 teaspoons salt
about 5 tablespoons olive oil
freshly ground black pepper
1 tablespoon finely chopped parsley

Cut up the chicken, first slicing through the skin above the leg down to the joint, then working the knife towards the tail, making a downward scoop with the knife to pick up the 'oyster' of flesh on the backbone. Cut both legs free through the joint. Cut off both wings, working from the backbone (keep them to use for stock).

Reach into the neck and find the wishbone with your fingers. Work along it with your first finger and thumb nails and pull it out. Cut down on either side of the breast bone and work the breasts free. Peel off all the skin and cut the flesh into bite-sized pieces. Halve the legs and take the flesh off the joints in big pieces, discarding a bony plate over the chicken's knee. This will give you about 350 g (12 oz) meat. Put this in a bowl.

Sprinkle the chopped garlic with a couple of teaspoons of salt and mash with the flat of the knife to a paste (or use a pestle and mortar). Work in 1 tablespoon of olive oil. Season the chicken pieces with pepper and stir in the garlic paste. Leave to marinate until needed, stirring occasionally.

Heat 4 tablespoons of olive oil in a frying pan and add the chicken pieces. Cook for about 10 minutes over medium-high heat until golden, turning them over with a spatula. Put a sheet of kitchen paper in the bottom of the serving dish, and transfer the chicken. Remove the paper, sprinkle with a little parsley and serve with a jar of cocktail sticks on the plate.

TARTALETAS DE RIÑONES AL JEREZ

TARTLETS OF KIDNEYS IN SHERRY

On most *tapas* bars in Spain you will find kidneys in sherry sauce – pigs' kidneys in tomato sauce in the poorer south, more sophisticated calf's or lambs' kidneys in the cities – a warming *ración* to stave off the pangs of hunger. At home kidney sauce is served with rice or even pasta and may well include cubes of ham or bacon in a sauce thickened with flour and vegetables.

This elegant version, with a few spoonfuls of sherry sauce, is served in small tartlets suitable for a drinks party. They should be eaten in two bites, so use small shallow tart tins, only 0.5 cm ($\frac{1}{4}$ in) deep, not the type sold for cup cakes.

SERVES 6 – 8

500 g (1 lb) calf's or lambs' kidneys
150 ml (5 fl oz) fino or amontillado sherry
2 tablespoons olive oil
2 tablespoons pork fat
1 garlic clove, finely chopped
1 tablespoon tomato paste
2 tablespoons finely chopped parsley, plus extra to garnish (optional)

PASTRY

75 g (3 oz) flour, plus extra for rolling
25 g (1 oz) semolina or coarse yellow cornmeal
65 g (2½ oz) unsalted butter, diced
¼ teaspoon salt
about 2 tablespoons lemon juice

Make the pastry: work the butter into the salted flour and semolina or cornmeal to make fine crumbs, then add enough lemon juice to make a smooth dough. Heat the oven to 180° C (350° F, gas 4) and grease 16 tart tins. Roll out the pastry, cut out circles with a biscuit cutter and line the tart tins. Bake for about 8 minutes.

CAFÉ The gentle click of dominoes is a typical sound in Spanish cafés, indispensable havens where people gather to eat and drink, discuss the world – or simply watch it go by.

To prepare the kidneys, remove all membrane, cut out the middle core and then cut into large dice. Heat the oil and pork fat in a frying pan and add the garlic. Over the highest heat put in the kidneys in handfuls, stirring them to seal cut surfaces. Pull them to the side and let the fat reheat before adding the next handful.

Add the sherry, stirring the kidneys gently as it reduces to about 4 tablespoons. Stir in the tomato paste and parsley and remove from the heat. Spoon into the tarts, sprinkle with a little more parsley if you wish and serve immediately.

CHAMPIÑONES RELLENOS

STUFFED MUSHROOMS

Quick to make, this is one of the few hot *tapas* that can be easily cooked in the middle of a drinks party. The recipe comes from Ana Diment Castillo at the Mesón Don Felipe in London. Hunt down your *chorizos* first, then buy button mushrooms of the right size to hold a slice of sausage when the stalk is removed.

SERVES 8

about 700 g (1½ lb) button mushrooms
4 cooking chorizos or fresh spicy sausages
salt
olive oil

Clean the mushrooms and remove the stems; salt the hollows lightly. Cut slices of *chorizo*, removing the skin, and push into the hollows. Brush the cap with oil, then place them cap side down on a baking tray.

Heat the grill to high. Grill them for 5 minutes until sizzling, and serve immediately.

BUÑUELOS DE QUESO

HOT FRIED CHEESE PUFFS

These puffs are much less interesting when they have been standing around – indeed *buñuelo* is slang for a 'bungle' or 'mess up' – so eat them almost immediately. To vary the batter, add 2 tablespoons of grated onion and a generous amount of cayenne pepper to the cheese. Alternatively, try 4 tablespoons of chopped almonds or green olives with, or instead of, the cheese.

SERVES 6

35 g (1½ oz) butter
¼ teaspoon salt
125 ml (4 fl oz) milk or water
65 g (2½ oz) flour, sifted
2 medium-sized eggs, beaten together
50 g (2 oz) Manchego cheese, or Parmesan or Gruyère, grated
½ teaspoon Dijon mustard
oil for deep frying
dusting of paprika or cayenne pepper

Put the butter, salt and milk in a pan and bring slowly to the boil. Off the heat add the flour and beat hard with a wooden spoon. Return to the heat and beat until the mixture forms a ball round the spoon – 1–2 minutes. Remove from the heat again and add the beaten eggs, beating to a smooth paste. Stir in the grated cheese and the mustard.

Heat the oil in a deep-fat fryer: to the top heat on an electric fryer, or until a bread cube will brown in 40 seconds. Using a teaspoon, and another to scrape it off, drop balls of mixture into the hot fat, 7–8 at a time. As soon as they pop to the surface, push them under with a slotted spoon, spinning them over. This helps them to colour evenly and form a good round shape as they double in size. Cook for about 5 minutes, until the outside is a dark gold and the inside no longer pasty. Drain on kitchen paper.

Serve the *buñuelos*, dusted with paprika or cayenne, with toothpicks to pick them up. A nutty, medium dry *amontillado* sherry is the ideal accompaniment.

BOQUERONES SIN TRABAJO

EFFORTLESS ANCHOVY SALAD

Black-backed fresh anchovies are caught all along the Mediterranean coast from Estepona on the Gibraltar road to Collioure over the French border. All they need is marinating and serving – hence the name – for a result totally unlike the canned fish.

SERVES 4

500 g (1 lb) fresh anchovies, or sardines or smelts
about ¾ teaspoon salt
about 150 ml (¼ pt) white wine vinegar
1 garlic clove, finely chopped
2 tablespoons chopped mild Spanish onion
3 tablespoons olive oil
2 teaspoons lemon juice
freshly ground black pepper
diced red pepper and chopped parsley to garnish (optional)

Cut off the heads and gut the fish, extending the cut beyond the stomach cavity as far as the tail. Turn each fish on to its belly and press your thumbs hard into the middle of the back: the fish will split open flat under pressure. Turn it over and pull out the backbone from the head end, snipping it free at the tail.

Lay the fish, skin down, in a shallow dish and sprinkle with the salt, vinegar, garlic and onion. Leave in a cool place for 24 hours.

The following day, drain and rinse the fish (reserving some onion). Pat dry with kitchen paper. Dress the fish with a vinaigrette made from oil, lemon juice and seasonings, then sprinkle with a little marinated onion, plus pepper and parsley for colour. Serve with chilled *fino* sherry as a *tapa* for a group, or with salad for lunch for three to four people.

MEDICINAL HERBS *A market in Granada sells herbs to guard against a variety of ailments – a more unusual use than their customary culinary one.*

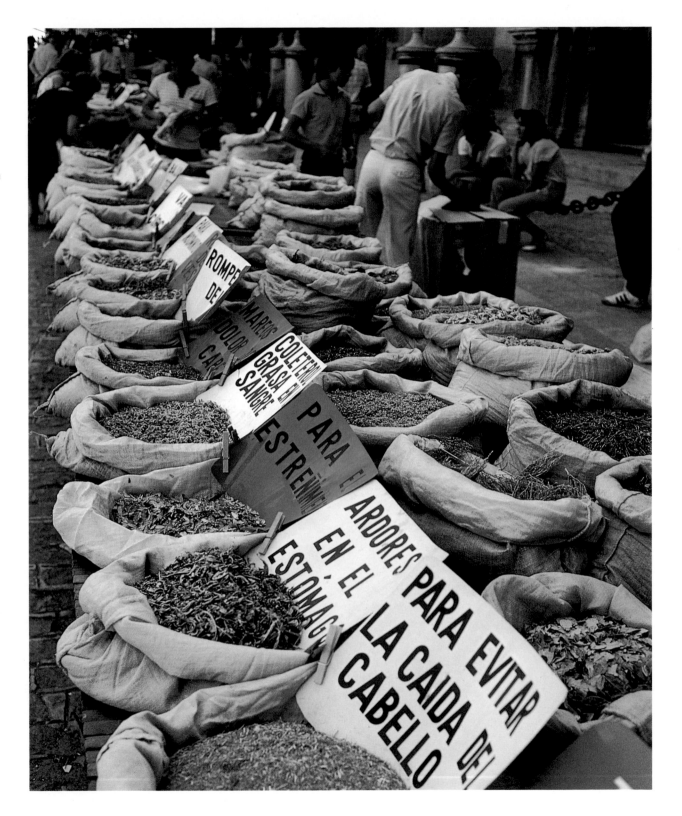

GAMBAS EN GABARDINAS

PRAWNS 'IN MACKINTOSHES'

Protected from the heat of the oil by a crisp coating of batter, these prawns are, literally translated, 'wearing mackintoshes'. It's the lightest and crispest fish batter that I know, and suitable only for ingredients that need little cooking. A pretty variation is to batter and fry a couple of strips of red pepper and 3 large green olives per person, with fewer prawns.

SERVES 4

500 g (1 lb) prawns in the shell
olive oil for deep frying
1 lemon, cut into wedges

FRITTER BATTER

100 g (4 oz) flour
pinch of salt
3 tablespoons oil or melted butter
175 ml (6 fl oz) tepid water
pinch of cayenne pepper
1 egg white

Make the batter: put the flour and salt in a bowl, stir in the oil or butter and gradually work in the warm water to make a paste then a smooth batter. Add a little cayenne. Let this stand while you peel the prawns. Remove the heads and shells, but leave the tail tip.

Heat the deep-frying oil (to top heat on an electric fryer), until it will crisp a bread cube in 30–40 seconds. When the oil is hot, whisk the egg white to soft peaks and fold it into the batter. Dip each prawn into the batter, holding it by the tail, and then drop into the oil. Let the prawns puff up and colour for about 30 seconds, then remove with a slotted spoon on to kitchen paper. Serve at once with the lemon wedges.

MEJILLONES CON PIMIENTO VERDE Y ROJO

COLD STUFFED MUSSELS WITH PEPPERS

The mussels of Galicia must be the best in the world – huge, sweet and bright orange like some strange fruit in a shell – and so tender they are eaten almost raw, just with lemon quarters. They are farmed in the western bays of the Atlantic coast, from little platforms with huts on top, that look like Chinese junks at sea.

In this simple recipe the mussels are gently steamed, then served with a crisp dice of red and green peppers, which adds colour and a new texture, making this a very attractive *tapa*.

Double the amounts given in the recipe for a starter for four people and double them again for a drinks party for 24, when people will probably only eat a couple of mussels each.

SERVES 4

500 g (1 lb) large mussels, cleaned (see page 96)
125 ml (4 fl oz) dry white wine
¼ green pepper
¼ red pepper
1–2 teaspoons lemon juice
salt and freshly ground black pepper

Heat the wine in a saucepan with a grinding of pepper, and put in a handful of mussels at a time. Steam them, covered, for 2–3 minutes. When open, fish them out and start removing top shells. Discard any that don't smell sweet or remain closed. Arrange the halves, 2 mussels in each shell, on a serving plate.

To remove any sand, strain the juices into a smaller pan through a butter muslin (or J-cloth) inside a sieve. Then boil to reduce to about 4 tablespoons of concentrated juice. Taste and season very carefully, adding a little lemon juice at a time, and salt and pepper if needed.

Use a coffee spoon to dribble a little juice over each mussel, just to glaze them. Dice the peppers very finely and sprinkle both colours in each shell. Chill until needed, but serve the same day.

A chilled white wine from Ribeiro is a natural

partner for this simple dish. This 'green' Albariño wine is flowery and somewhat acid: one of Spain's best fish wines. It is usually slightly sparkling, in the style of *vinho verde* from Portugal, which is made from the same grapes, just over the border. However the Spanish wines will seem drier, as the Portuguese wines are sweetened for export. Best known is Palacio de Fefiñanes, which is not sparkling.

Only coat the second batch while the first fish are frying, so the flour has no chance of becoming wet. Fry all the fish, in 5–6 batches, draining each batch on clean kitchen paper. Sprinkle with cayenne and serve immediately with lemon wedges to squeeze over them.

Strain the oil immediately after use, then heat a long strip of lemon zest in it to remove the fishy smell. Even after this, keep the oil for fish only.

CHANQUETES

DEEP-FRIED WHITEBAIT

Tiny, transparent fish called *chanquetes* swim, sometimes in huge banks, off the southern coast of Spain – the *fideos* or thin spaghetti of the sea. Such fish, as well as others like baby anchovies and sardines, are deep-fried – an art at which Spaniards excel. Although they are often fried in batter (see page 26), flour makes the better coating for fish as thick as whitebait, our closest equivalent to *chanquetes*.

SERVES 4

500 g (1 lb) very fresh whitebait
4 tablespoons flour
½ teaspoon salt
freshly ground black pepper
dusting of cayenne pepper
olive oil for deep frying
wedges of lemon to serve

Rinse the fish and pat dry with plenty of kitchen paper. Heat enough oil for deep frying to 190°C (375°F) – top temperature on an electric fryer and just below smoking point for olive oil. A bread cube should crisp in 30–40 seconds.

Put the flour and seasonings in a plastic bag and add a handful of fish. Shake to coat them, then remove the fish to a plate; this minimizes the amount of flour that goes into the fryer. Add the fish to the hot oil and fry for 1½–2 minutes until lightly golden. Faint blisters will appear on the sides of the fish. Remove with a slotted spoon to kitchen paper to drain.

GAMBAS PIL-PIL

SIZZLING CHILLI-HOT PRAWNS

These prawns are immensely popular, not least because this is a good way of disguising previously cooked, and even frozen, prawns. The recipe below is for serving with drinks, but the dish is often made as a starter, in individual dishes. Small *cazuelitas* are heated in the oven and each person is then given at least 4–5 tablespoons of oil with the prawns. Heavily flavoured with chilli, the oil is a popular part of the dish. The little pots are carried to the table, each covered by a piece of bread to stop the oil spitting, and the bread then serves to mop up the oil.

SERVES 4

250–350 g (8–12 oz) peeled prawns, defrosted if frozen
2 garlic cloves
2 dried chillies or 1 fresh one, stalk and seeds removed, or ¼–1 teaspoon chilli powder
pinch of paprika
6–7 tablespoons olive oil

Crush the garlic cloves with the flat of a knife. Heat the oil in a frying pan with the garlic and sliced fresh chilli, if using, or dried chilli or powder. When the garlic browns, discard it and the dried chilli; a fresh chilli should remain in the pan.

Blot the prawns well with kitchen paper if they are defrosted, toss in very hot oil for a minute or so and sprinkle with paprika. Serve in a very hot dish with the oil and fresh chilli and eat with cocktail sticks.

MANTECA COLORADA

PAPRIKA PORK RILLETTES

This is a good help-yourself appetizer for a group of people sitting together, with a bottle of wine, watching the sun go down and lazily waiting for dinner. Textured with little shreds of pork, the soft red pork fat is rather similar to the *sobrasada* sausage, sold in and out of its skin, so popular in Mallorca.

SERVES 8

400 g (14 oz) pork back fat without rind
400 g (14 oz) pork belly
3 fat garlic cloves
6 tablespoons fino *sherry*
2 bay leaves, crumbled
2 tablespoons paprika
plenty of freshly grated nutmeg
1 teaspoon salt
plenty of freshly ground black pepper

Heat the oven to 140° C (275° F, gas 1). Cube the fat as small as you can. Cut the belly into rectangles following the grain of the meat, so that there will be 2.5 cm, (1 in) shreds of pork later. Put the meat and fat cubes into a casserole warming on the stove. Crush the garlic cloves with the flat side of a knife and add to the casserole with the sherry.

Move the covered casserole to the oven for 1 hour, then stir and season well with the herbs and spices. Stir again then cook very gently for about 5 hours (this is a good partner in the oven for meringues).

Turn into a colander over a heatproof bowl. Press the fat with the back of a spoon, then pick the meat cubes to pieces with two forks, adding the shredded meat to the liquid fat in the bowl. Discard what is left of the cubes. Taste the liquid fat to check the seasonings. In Spain this is packed into the same tall straight-sided brown terracotta pots that are used for yoghurt. It makes about 450 ml (16 fl oz). Chill until needed then serve with French bread.

PA AMB TOMÀQUET CON JAMÓN Y QUESO

TOMATO BREAD WITH RAW HAM AND CHEESE

In Catalonia bread is rarely put on the table without an accompanying tomato. When the summers are hot – and the tomatoes therefore superior – I eat Catalan tomato bread for lunch almost every day, for it makes the ideal foil to salad. It's both delicious and economical – a similar idea to the *chaponnade* of garlic bread in the bottom of a Provençal salad bowl. Here it's topped with Spain's best raw ham and cheese.

SERVES 8

1 long French loaf
700 g (1½ lb) ripe red tomatoes
6–8 garlic cloves
jug containing 125 ml (4 fl oz) olive oil
about 250 g (8 oz) jamón serrano *or* prosciutto, *sliced thinly*
about 300 g (10 oz) Manchego cheese or young Parmesan, sliced thinly

Slice the French bread diagonally and cut the ham and cheese into pieces no larger than the bread. Arrange on two plates. Put everything on the table together with side plates and knives. Toast the bread very lightly.

To eat, each person cuts a tomato in half and squeezes the tomato juice on to each side of the toast. Next, halve the garlic cloves and wipe the cut side on to the juice. Finally, sprinkle a teaspoon or so of olive oil on top. *Aficionados*, especially in the Val d'Arran in the Pyrenees, will eat it just like this, but the more sophisticated version is to top the toasts with a slice each of raw ham and cheese.

SQUARE IN LÉRIDA *The morning's shopping is interrupted by a chat in the town square, invariably the hub around which Spanish towns and villages revolve.*

OLIVE TREES IN ANDALUSIA (overleaf) *Seemingly endless olive groves stretch as far as the eye can see – a typical landscape in Andalusia, whose parched, arid land is particularly suited to olive-growing.*

GAZPACHO ROJO
DE SEVILLA

SEVILLIAN CHILLED RED SOUP

Gazpacho dates back to before Roman times, in origin a primitive soup with the chill of cold stone floors and icy well water. Foreigners looked down on it as a provincial dish – *caspa* is Italian for 'remains' or 'bits', *acho* is derogatory. Fame came in the 19th century, after peppers, cucumbers and tomatoes were added.

Spaniards say there are 'as many different *gazpachos* as there are mortars and pestles' and how a cook prepares it betrays his or her regional origin. The Madrid version includes mayonnaise and others may include morsels of game and stock. In winter it is a hot soup, even a thick one. But it is at its best and most refreshing served chilled, in hot weather.

SERVES 6

2 slices stale white bread, without crusts
1 small onion, roughly chopped
2 garlic cloves, finely chopped
250 g (8 oz) red pepper (green if using tomato juice), without stalk or seeds
500 g (1 lb) ripe red tomatoes, without skin or seeds, or 400 g (14 oz) canned, sieved tomatoes, with juice, or 750 ml (1¼ pt) tomato juice (omitting half the iced water later)
1 cucumber, half the skin and all the seeds removed
2 tablespoons sherry vinegar or red wine vinegar
2 tablespoons olive oil
1 teaspoon coarse salt
pinch of cayenne pepper
850 ml (1½ pt) iced water

GARNISH
a selection from the following:
4 tablespoons freshly fried croûtons
4 tablespoons chopped pepper, red or green
2 hard-boiled eggs, peeled and chopped
4 tablespoons chopped mild Spanish onion or spring onions
a handful of green or black olives, stoned and chopped

AJO BLANCO CON UVAS DE MÁLAGA *top*, GAZPACHO ROJO DE SEVILLA *bottom*.

Cover the bread with water, then squeeze it out. Put the bread, onion, garlic and cayenne in a blender with the oil and salt and purée everything. Add the cucumber, pepper, vinegar and the tomato or juice. You will probably have to make it in two batches.

Chill for at least 12 hours, preferably overnight, turning the refrigerator down to its lowest setting, or put it in the freezer for about 30 minutes.

Before serving, dilute with iced water – though preferably don't serve with ice cubes in it. Arrange the garnishes in little dishes and pass them around on a tray.

AJO BLANCO CON UVAS
DE MÁLAGA

CHILLED ALMOND SOUP,
MALAGA-STYLE, WITH GRAPES

White *gazpacho* goes back at least 1000 years, to the time when Moors ruled much of Spain. It was originally made by pounding almonds with icy well water and was particularly soothing in the heat of the Andalusian summer. This is the more sophisticated, creamy *Malagueñan* version, with a sweet grape garnish.

SERVES 4–5

250 g (8 oz) white stale bread or rolls, without crusts
2 garlic cloves, peeled
pinch of salt
2–3 tablespoons olive oil
2 tablespoons sherry vinegar or white wine vinegar
100 g (4 oz) sealed packet of ground almonds
600 ml (1 pt) iced water
250 g (8 oz) white grapes, seeded

Pour water over the bread, then squeeze it out. Tear into pieces and put them in a blender with the garlic cloves. Add the salt and olive oil, and purée everything.

Add the vinegar and almonds with enough iced water to blend until smooth. Slowly add the remaining water with the blender running, to make a cream. Chill for at least 2 hours. Check the seasonings, ladle into bowls and garnish with grapes.

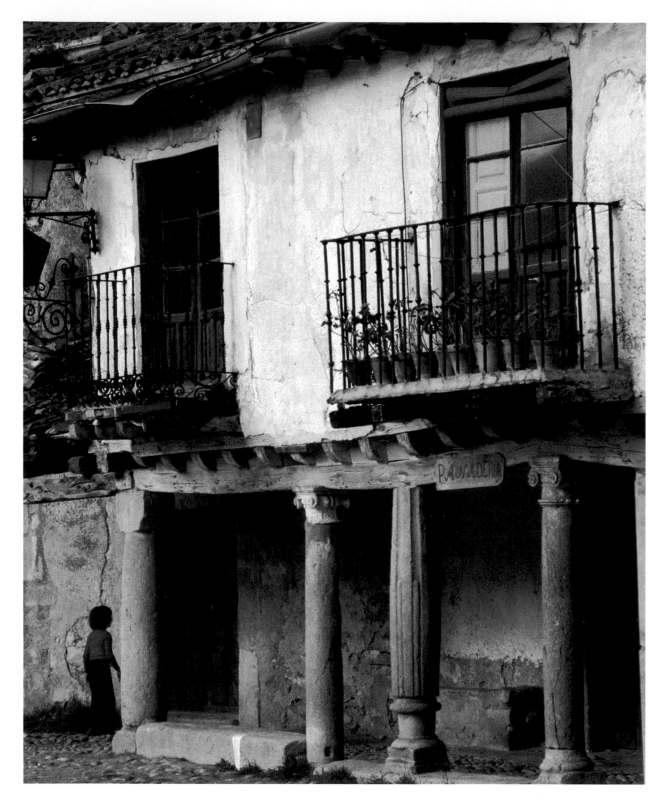

SOPA DE AJO CON HUEVOS

GARLIC SOUP
WITH POACHED EGGS

All over Spain people eat garlic soups – from the humble varieties, like beggars' soup in Avila, made only from fried garlic and breadcumbs, coloured with paprika and diluted with salt water, to richer ones – like the soup of 'bread, garlic, paprika and beaten egg', which Alexandre Dumas thought worth recording on his journey through Castile in the 1840s. In La Mancha a similar soup is served to lovers on their wedding night to 'raise their morale'.

SERVES 4

*2 thick slices of country-style (not packet) bread,
without crusts
2 tablespoons olive oil
4 garlic cloves, finely chopped
1 teaspoon paprika
850 ml (1½ pt) light stock or water
salt
4 eggs*

Heat the oven to 165°C (325°F, gas 3) with 4 individual casseroles or ovenproof soup plates. Fry the bread in oil in the bottom of a casserole, with the garlic in one corner, making sure it doesn't burn. After turning the bread, sprinkle the top with paprika. Remove the bread and garlic to a blender and purée with a little stock or water. Return to the casserole and add the remaining stock or water – adding more salt if water alone is used. Bring to the boil.

Break the eggs into the soup plates and ladle in the soup. Pop them in the oven for about 8 minutes to allow the eggs to set slightly. If you don't want to heat the oven just for this, the eggs can be beaten into the hot soup.

BAKER'S SHOP IN CASTILE *Panadería points to a bakery in this somewhat unlikely setting. No Spanish table would be complete without crusty, freshly baked bread to accompany the meal and Castile, where conditions are perfect for wheat-growing, is said to produce Spain's finest.*

SOPA DE PICADILLO

CLEAR SOUP WITH HAM,
EGG AND MINT

I like the clear fresh taste of mint and ham in this soup. *Picadillo* usually means minced meat, but ham is the traditional garnish for this soup, which is made from *caldo de puchero*, broth from the stockpot. In former times, this broth was a standard item, at least in meat-eating households, for meats were boiled at least once a week for dishes like *cocido madrileño* (see page 104). And very good it is too, with no vegetable flavours, just distilled meat essences. Famous soups, like *consomé al Jerez*, sherried consommé, are based on it. Bad broths, of course, exist. Richard Ford clearly ate one in the 1840s when he commented that the stockpot, or *'olla* is made of 2 cigars boiled in 3 gallons of water'.

I use chicken stock made with carcasses, but try to include a gammon knuckle bone, often its second cooking, and some chickpeas when making it.

SERVES 4

*1 l (1¾ pt) light meat or chicken stock
100 g (4 oz) raw ham or smoked gammon, cubed
2 hard-boiled eggs, chopped
leaves from 4 sprigs of mint*

Heat the stock with the chopped ham. Check the seasoning, add the mint and chopped egg and serve.

PURRUSALDA

LEEK AND POTATO SOUP

The name of this soup comes from leeks, *puerros*, and *saldo*, meaning 'well-balanced' and also the name of a local Basque dance. Sometimes the soup contains *bacalao*, or salt cod. This is soaked and briefly fried, and the soup is then made with water, rather than stock.

SERVES 6

4 leeks, keeping a little of the green tops (about 500 g [1 lb] after trimming)
500 g (1 lb) potatoes, sliced very thinly, then quartered if large
2 garlic cloves, finely chopped
2 tablespoons pork or chicken fat, or butter
salt and white pepper
650 ml (1 pt 2 fl oz) meat or chicken stock
toast to serve

The easiest way to clean leeks is to split them half through lengthways, then turn them upside down in a jug of cold water. After 10 minutes, drain and cut them into rings.

Sweat the leeks in hot fat until they collapse. Add the potatoes and garlic, season with salt and pepper, and fry for a moment, stirring gently. Pour in the stock and cook for 15–20 minutes. Check the seasoning and serve with bread toasted in the oven.

Soup made with meat stock is best eaten freshly made and is sometimes served with a crust of grilled cheese on top. A cream soup can be made if you use chicken stock: increase the amount of liquid slightly and then purée it.

PURRUSALDA

CALDO GALLEGO

GALICIAN CABBAGE SOUP

A warming soup for the cold, opening months of the year, *caldo gallego* also has a spring freshness. It is so popular outside Galicia that all the items for it are sold specially in Madrid. Traditionally it's made with *grelos*, the top spring leaves of turnips, with the buds just coming into flower, though the side shoots of cabbage are used instead in the Basque country. The new potatoes are special too – called *cachelos*.

The other constituent is salted meat. The old way of the farmer's wife was to use an *unto* – a bacon bone aged for at least 5 years, with a little *tocino*. Sometimes translated as 'bacon', this word embraces the salt-cured ribs of pork belly and a great deal of fat. I've used fresh spare ribs successfully; or use salt pork belly, whichever is easiest.

SERVES 6

250 g (8 oz) dried haricot beans
350 g (12 oz) pork belly ribs or
125 g (5 oz) salt pork
500 g (1 lb) smoked gammon knuckle bone with a little meat attached
500 g (1 lb) potatoes, egg-sized
200 g (7 oz) tender turnip leaves or kale
salt and freshly ground black pepper

Pour boiling water over the beans and leave to soak for an hour. If using pork ribs, rub them well with salt. If using salt pork, put it into a pan with the gammon bone, cover with cold water and bring to boiling point. Simmer for 5 minutes then drain. Cube the salt pork.

Put the gammon, pork bones or cubed pork and drained beans into a casserole and cover with 2 l (3½ pt) water. Bring to simmering point, skim off any scum, then cook gently, covered, for 1 hour.

Add the halved potatoes and simmer for another 20 minutes. Prepare the greens, removing thicker stems. Remove all the bones from the pot and check the stock for salt and pepper. Add the greens to the pot and simmer for another 5 – 10 minutes. Meanwhile, remove all the edible meat from the bones and return it to the pan. To thicken the liquid a little, fish out a few potatoes, mash and return them.

CALDILLO DE PERRO

CADIZ FISH SOUP WITH ORANGE

The affection in which this winter soup is held is indicated by the diminutive 'little soup'. *Perro* means 'dog' and the soup comes from the fishermen's quarters at Puerto de Santa Maria, which commands the incomparable Cadiz harbour. There is also a 'cat' soup – though perversely it is fishless.

SERVES 6

1 kg (2 lb) young hake, probably 3 fish, filleted, with the heads, bones and belly trimmings
5 garlic cloves
1 large onion, finely chopped
2 tablespoons olive oil
juice of 4 Seville oranges or 3 sweet ones
2 lemons (if using sweet oranges)
1 orange, peeled, sliced and quartered
2 teaspoons salt
freshly ground black pepper

Cut the hake fillets into slices 7.5 cm (3 in) long and sprinkle the cut side with the salt. The flesh of immature hake is very soft and pink (unlike mature fish) and salt stiffens it. The belly cavity is unusual in being lined with a thick black skin and the quickest way to fillet (especially for soup) is to confine the fillets to the upper sides and backs of the fish.

Put the heads, bones and belly trimmings into a saucepan and add 1.2 l (2 pt) water and a spiral of zest from one orange. Bring to simmering point, skim, then simmer, covered, for 30 minutes.

Crush the garlic cloves with the flat of a knife. Heat the oil in a soup pot over high heat and add the garlic. When the cloves colour, discard them and turn down the heat. Fry the onion gently until softened, then strain in the hot fish stock and bring back to the boil.

Add the hake pieces, a few at a time, without letting the soup go off the boil. Cook for 15 – 20 minutes, add the juice from the oranges (and lemon) and check the seasoning. Garnish with quartered orange slices.

SHEEP IN GALICIA *The black sheep lives up to its reputation and strikes out alone in the lush green countryside of Galicia.*

EGGS, RICE
AND PASTA

The simple, delicious staples of eggs and rice are indispensable to the country food of Spain and the more modern pasta has introduced a new note into traditional cooking.

PAELLA VALENCIANA *(p 53)*.

EGGS ARE THE FOOD OF country folk – as in Ireland, in earlier times in Spain much was measured by the value of an egg. Egg dishes are still very much a basic part of Spanish cuisine, listed as a separate course on the menu. These are country dishes, making good use of small amounts of food, gathered fresh that morning from the garden plot, when the hen's egg was also retrieved warm from the place where she hid it.

Rice is treated in the same way, flavoured by small additions of vegetables, pork or seafood. It has been part of the Spanish diet since the Arabs introduced it to Valencia in the 9th century, on land the Romans had irrigated. It's a basic food in the south, stuffed into vegetables, accompanying stews and forming the base of salads. The Catalans bake it as *arròs passejat*, meaning 'walked rice', for in the past it went out of the house to be cooked in the baker's oven. The north of Spain, however, accepted rice first as a milk pudding.

Spain's most famous rice dish, *paella*, is firmly based in Valencia on the east coast and is probably only two centuries old. It comes from La Huerta, meaning 'the market garden', near Lake Albufera to the south of the city. This is one of the largest freshwater lakes in Spain and the home of delicious eels. So the original *paella* may well have been a Lenten mixture of eels, snails and vegetables like *garrafones*, the local white beans. It was cooked out-of-doors over a fire of vine prunings and *paella* is still the most enchanting of outdoor foods. The saffron-gold of the rice is flecked with red, green and pink and the different shapes of shellfish, and each of the small surprises it contains has a new flavour and texture.

Paella is traditionally a dish cooked by men – outside, as barbecues are – with preparations shared pleasantly over a bottle of wine. A group of people, though, means the shallow pan must be a big one – 40 cm (15 in) across and sometimes more. Such pans need low heat, ideally as wide as the pan, and out-of-doors hot charcoal can be spread out to provide this. This is not so easy to manage indoors, though a heat diffuser works well.

Big *paellas* are often cooked in the oven from the point when all the stock is included and they have been stirred for the last time. However, this rules out one of the charms of a garden *paella*: the *socarrat*, a toasted golden crust at the bottom of the pan. The best *paella* pans have a dimpled bottom to prevent this sticking.

To outsiders, Valencian *paella* is known for its chicken and seafood mixture, but this famous dish has many local versions. *Arròs en perdiu*, rice with 'partridge', is a Lenten dish from the same province. It includes chickpeas with the rice and, as meat was forbidden during Lent, the bird of the title is in fact a whole bulb of garlic.

Paellas are cooked until all the liquid has been absorbed by the rice, when the rice becomes 'dry'. But the Valencia area also has soupy rice dishes, *arroces caldosos*, which are cooked in the *caldero* pot like many famous fish stews on both the north and east coasts. Very often these are fishy rice stews, bolstered with vegetables and a little *ñora* chilli, which is popular on the Alicante coast. Beans and turnips are the backbone of the Valencian *arròs amb fesols i naps*, but this also includes pork in the form of pig's ears, a trotter and blood sausage, and is cooked in the traditional *olla*.

Paellas can absorb everything the countryside has to offer: frog and rabbit, game birds and chicken have all become constituents of *paella*. There are game *paellas* and, more modestly, vegetable ones, though almost all of them are usually flavoured with various parts and products of the pig.

The best-loved *paellas*, however, are those containing seafood and there is a natural affinity between them and fish. The key to a *paella*'s success is a splendid stock. It is both aesthetic and practical, therefore, to start with fish stock, since fish produce so much debris that cannot be used in any other way than for soup.

The introduction of pasta to Spain has given rise to what appears to be a new *paella* seafood dish, the *fideuà*, in which pasta has replaced the traditional rice. Pasta has become popular generally and a big factory in Malaga produces it for the south and east. It is cooked in two main ways. *Fideos*, a very short spaghetti, comes in various thicknesses that go into soups. Like the rest of us, the Spaniards also make macaroni cheese. A great influx of Italian chefs in the 19th century spread ideas such as cheese sauce and introduced *canelones* to Spain. Cannelloni is now a popular dish, eaten on Saint Stephen's Day (the day after Christmas), though the cannelloni tube is still not on sale. The local version is half-sheets of lasagne, bought in packets, then cooked and rolled at home.

TORTILLA ESPAÑOLA

SPANISH POTATO OMELETTE

Invented by a peasant for a hungry king, so the story goes, the *tortilla* has been made for at least 400 years – a dense moist cake of egg, totally different from the French omelette. *Tortillas* with potato have been a favourite since the 18th century, but they can contain anything you fancy. In the following recipe the potato could be replaced by 250 g (8 oz) onions, softened until golden, or fat prawns, or spoonfuls of *samfaina* (see page 88).

There are only two rules. The first is that the contents must not greatly exceed the volume of eggs, and the second is that the additions must not drip – either with sauce or with oil. Serve *tortillas* hot, warm or cold. This recipe will make a starter for four people or supper for two.

SERVES 4

500 g (1 lb) potatoes, peeled and diced
6 large eggs
125 ml (4 fl oz) olive oil
salt and freshly ground black pepper

Don't use too large a frying pan – a pan about 23 cm (9 in) across with sides is needed to produce a sponge-cake shape with vertical sides. Heat a generous quantity of oil until very hot, add the potatoes and stir them so they are coated with oil. Reduce the heat and let the potatoes cook through, turning them over frequently so they do not colour.

Use a slotted spoon to move the potatoes to a bowl with a layer of kitchen paper at the bottom. Drain the oil from the pan into a cup and wipe out the pan with paper if there are any sticky or crusty patches.

Strain about 2 tablespoons of oil back into the pan, and reheat. Beat the eggs together and season them well. Pull the paper from under the potatoes and pour the eggs over them, so they are well coated. Pour the mixture into the hot oil, spreading the potatoes evenly, and give it a minute at high heat to set, before turning down the heat. Use a spatula to pull the *tortilla* off the sides of the pan to make an upright edge, shaking the pan to and fro occasionally, to make sure the bottom isn't catching.

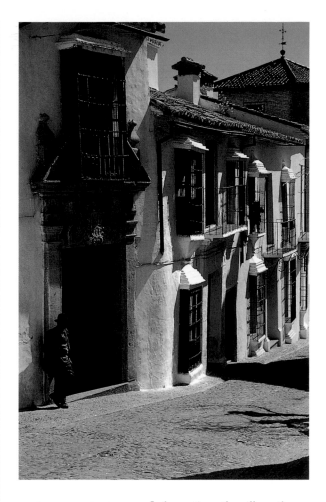

WROUGHT-IRON GRILLES *In former times, the grilles on these houses in Andalusia protected the daughter of the house sitting within from the attentions of her admirer, wooing her from the other side.*

When the top has ceased to be liquid, cover with a serving plate and invert the pan to turn the *tortilla* out. Add 2 more tablespoons of oil, return the *tortilla* to the pan – cooked side up – and cook for a further 2–3 minutes. Serve hot, alone or with tomato sauce or *samfaina* (see page 88).

Some people like it even better cold: in a thick wedge with a salad of tomato and mint, or cut in cubes and served as a *tapa* on a stick. Traditionally, poor farm workers took a chunk of *tortilla*, sandwiched in a *bocadillo*, to the fields for their midday meal. Once cooked, a *tortilla* will keep for a couple of days and even reheats well in tomato sauce.

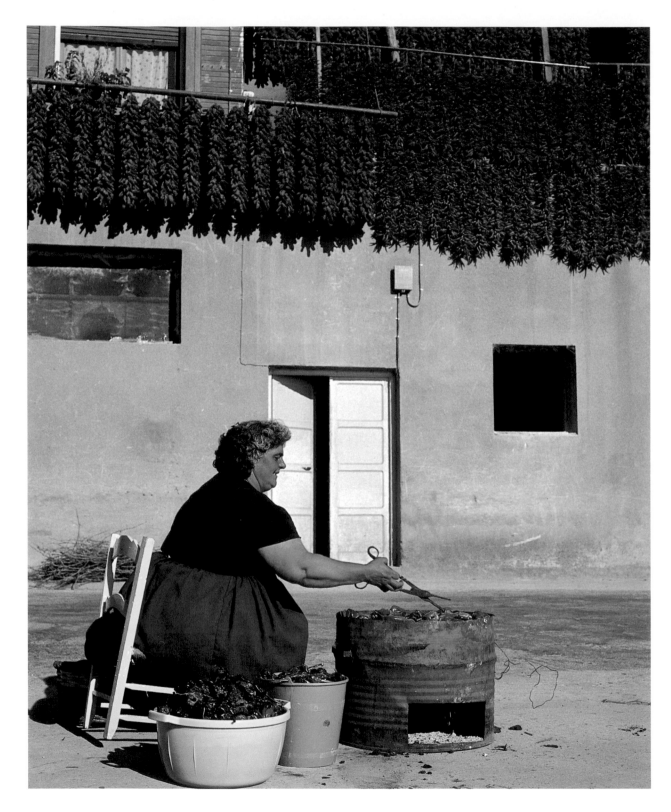

PIPERRADA VASCA

BASQUE PEPPER OMELETTE

There are many chopped vegetable sauces in the Spanish repertoire, but this one has a creamy French sophistication – not surprising since it comes from the Basque country, half of which is in France. The texture is achieved by grilling and skinning the peppers beforehand, so they are soft enough to melt into the eggs. The cold mixture also makes a very good filling for a *bocadillo* sandwich.

SERVES 4

500 g (1 lb) peppers, red or green
500 g (1 lb) ripe tomatoes, without skin or seeds,
or 400 g (14 oz) canned tomatoes, drained
6 large eggs
4 tablespoons oil
1 onion, chopped
1 garlic clove, finely chopped
4 slices of ham or back bacon
salt and freshly ground black pepper

Grill the peppers whole for about 20 minutes, giving them a quarter turn every 5 minutes, until they are charred on all sides. Transfer them to a plastic bag for 10 minutes.

Meanwhile heat 2 tablespoons of oil in a frying pan and cook the onion slowly until golden, adding the garlic near the end. Chop the tomato flesh (or pulse briefly in a processor) and add to the pan. Remove the skin from the peppers, discarding stalks and seeds, and chop (or process briefly). Add to the pan and cook to a soft sauce.

Beat the eggs together, season and pour over the vegetables, stirring them together to make a soft, creamy, orange-coloured mixture, then fry like a French omelette without stirring. Fry the ham or bacon in 2 tablespoons of oil and serve together.

CHORICERO CHILLIES *In this Rioja village a brazier is used to char peppers, prior to skinning them. Hanging out to dry on the wall behind are glorious red bundles of sweet chillies,* choriceros, *which give their colour, taste and name to* chorizo *sausages.*

REVUELTO DE ESPÁRRAGOS TRIGUEROS

SCRAMBLED EGGS WITH YOUNG ASPARAGUS

'Everyone who has visited southern Spain in the spring', says Gerald Brenan in *South from Granada*, 'will have sampled the thin, bitter asparagus. This is never planted in gardens, but is picked from a tall thorny plant that grows on every mountain slope in southern Spain that is not too far from the sea.' I have never picked it myself, but in April I have met people with bundles of *trigueros* under their arms while I was hunting for bee-orchids, which share the same season. Since then the two have always been pleasantly connected in my mind.

Revuelto means stirred, but 'soft-set' is a better description of these eggs. The Spaniards scramble eggs in a frying pan and make the distinction between eggs that are stirred while cooking, which remain soft underneath, and *tortillas*, which set to a golden crust (see page 43).

SERVES 4

350 g (12 oz) thin green asparagus
8 large eggs
2 tablespoons butter
2 tablespoons olive oil
2 tablespoons milk
salt and freshly ground black pepper

Scrape the asparagus from below the bud to the base, removing points and the stringy outside of the stems. Cook in boiling water in a wide casserole (or in a roasting tin on top of the stove if they are long) until almost soft. This will take 8 – 10 minutes for cultivated asparagus: wild asparagus is hard and bitter and needs 30 minutes and a change of water.

Drain the asparagus and cut into 4 cm (1½ in) lengths, discarding tough ends. Heat the butter in two frying pans until frothing, then turn the asparagus in the hot fat. Beat the rest of the ingredients together and pour in. Turn up to medium-high heat and scramble the eggs lightly, stirring the outside to the middle with a wooden spoon. Serve this lovely creamy spring dish with crusty bread.

REVUELTO CON SETAS

SCRAMBLED EGGS WITH WILD MUSHROOMS

The better the quality of the mushrooms in this dish, the less egg is used – just enough to bind them together when wild mushrooms are in season. If button mushrooms are substituted, use an extra egg. The dish is best made in a non-stick pan.

SERVES 2

250 g (8 oz) oyster or fresh shiitake *mushrooms*
3 large eggs
2 tablespoons butter
1 tablespoon olive oil
1 garlic clove, finely chopped
1 tablespoon milk
salt and freshly ground black pepper
1 tablespoon finely chopped parsley

Heat the butter and oil in a frying pan until foaming. Add the garlic and the sliced mushrooms and cook over medium heat, turning occasionally with a wooden spoon, until they are soft. If they give off juice, turn up the heat and boil it away.

Beat the eggs with the milk, seasoning and parsley, and add to the pan. Cook over medium heat, pulling the eggs to the middle until just set. Serve at once.

HUEVOS A LA FLAMENCA

COLOURFUL BAKED EGGS

With its swirl of red, green, yellow and white, this dish has all the vibrant colour of the whirling skirts of gipsy dancers. Prawns can be substituted for the sausage, or everything included in a grand medley.

SERVES 4

1 large onion, chopped
2 garlic cloves, finely chopped
4 tablespoons olive oil
100 g (4 oz) cooking chorizo *or fresh spicy sausage,*
sliced, or smoked gammon or bacon, cubed
2 red or green peppers (350 g [12 oz]), chopped
350 g (12 oz) ripe tomatoes, without skin or seeds, or
300 g (10 oz) canned tomatoes, with juice
100 g (4 oz) peas
100 g (4 oz) French beans, snapped in short lengths
8 large eggs
1 – 2 tablespoons fino *or amontillado* sherry
salt
pinch of cayenne pepper

Heat the oven to 180° C (350° F, gas 4) and warm a shallow casserole or baking dish.

Heat the oil in a frying pan and soften the onion slowly. Add the garlic and push to the sides of the pan, then fry the sausage or ham until coloured and remove it. Add the peppers and chopped tomato to the pan and let them cook and reduce, stirring occasionally. Add some sherry if the mixture seems dry. Meanwhile cook the peas and beans and add them too.

Transfer the vegetable mixture to the casserole and distribute the sausage or ham. Swirl the eggs together with a fork without overmixing, seasoning them well with cayenne and salt. Pour over the vegetables and meat and bake in the oven for about 10 – 15 minutes until the eggs are just set.

HUEVOS A LA FLAMENCA

CHALK SOIL IN GRANADA (overleaf) *The lime-green shades in this starkly impressive Andalusian landscape indicate chalky soil, which, further west in Jerez, produces ideal conditions for the cultivation of sherry grapes.*

PISTO MANCHEGO CON HUEVOS FRITOS

TOMATO STEW
WITH DEEP-FRIED EGGS

A pleasant starter from La Mancha, Don Quixote country in central Spain, which makes a good supper dish. Use pumpkin towards the end of the year and courgettes, or 250 g (8 oz) green beans, in summer. Beans will need 3–4 tablespoons of stock too, as they take up moisture rather than adding it.

Deep-fried eggs will be a surprise to anyone who has not eaten them – they are deliciously light, puffy and digestible. It's worth making double the amout of *pisto*, if you have time, for it makes an excellent sauce to serve with poultry or for reheating rice.

SERVES 3 – 4

2 green peppers (about 250 g [8 oz]), seeded and chopped
500 g (1 lb) ripe tomatoes, without skin or seeds, or 400 g (14 oz) canned tomatoes, with juice
350 g (12 oz) cubed courgettes (unpeeled) or pumpkin
2 onions (about 250 g [8 oz]), chopped
2 garlic cloves, finely chopped
75 g (3 oz) smoked back bacon, in strips
1 – 2 eggs per person
2 tablespoons oil
salt and freshly ground black pepper
pinch of freshly ground nutmeg
olive oil for deep frying eggs
1 – 2 tablespoons finely chopped parsley

Heat the oil in a frying pan or casserole and soften the onion with the bacon, adding the garlic towards the end. Add the peppers and fry for 5 minutes. Add the tomatoes with their juice, and the courgette or pumpkin and cook over low heat, stirring occasionally and mashing with a spoon until reduced to a thick sauce. This will take about 20 minutes for courgettes, 35 for pumpkin. Season well, adding rather more nutmeg if you are using pumpkin.

Next fry the eggs. Heat olive oil, about 1.5 cm ($\frac{1}{2}$ in) deep, in a saucepan until hot. Break one egg at a time into a cup, slipping the egg into the centre of the oil, then tip the saucepan to make a deep-frying pool at the edge. At the same time roll the white round the egg with a skimmer or slotted spoon. It only takes 10 seconds to produce a puffy egg, so lift it out almost immediately.

Arrange the deep-fried eggs on the *pisto* and season lightly. Garnish the dish with a little finely chopped parsley and serve.

HUEVOS ESCALFADOS CON ALMEJAS

POACHED EGGS WITH CLAM SAUCE

This recipe, which originally came from the Poor Clares community of nuns, illustrates beautifully how humble food from one place can seem almost glamorous in another context. Mussels or cockles can also be used instead of the clams.

SERVES 4

1 kg (2 lb) clams, washed
1 onion, chopped
4 large fresh eggs
250 ml (8 fl oz) fish stock, canned clam juice, or
clam-and-tomato juice
175 ml (6 fl oz) dry white wine
3 garlic cloves, finely chopped
3 tablespoons chopped parsley
2 tablespoons butter
1 tablespoon flour
salt and freshly ground black pepper
vinegar for poaching
4 tostadas – slices of toasted or fried bread

Wash the clams in fresh water, discarding open ones. Heat the stock and wine with the chopped onion in a large pan with a lid. Put in enough clams to cover the bottom, cover and steam for a minute or so. When they open, scoop them out with a slotted spoon into a flameproof casserole, throw more clams into the pan and repeat. If they are small, pull off as many unoccupied top shells as you can. Reserve the liquid.

Put the butter into a saucepan and, when it is hot, stir in the garlic and parsley. Don't let the garlic colour, but add the flour, stirring to cook it. Add the liquid from the clam pan, a little at a time, simmer gently, taste and season. Pour this sauce over the clams and let them simmer for about 5 minutes.

Meanwhile, poach the eggs. Break the eggs individually into a cup and add one at a time to a wide pan of boiling water, with a few drops of vinegar (or use a poacher). Use a skimmer or slotted spoon to wrap the white round the yolk – the eggs will take about 4 minutes each to cook.

Put a *tostada* in each soup plate or dish, top with an egg and cover with clams and sauce. Large clams with both shells can be arranged round the egg, like the petals of a waterlily, but a sauce full of small ones is more traditional. When eating, use your tongue to scoop the clam off the shell and then spit out the latter.

WINDMILLS IN LA MANCHA *Don Quixote's stark, treeless tableland, bathed in shimmering, mysterious light, is punctuated only by the windmills which so readily evoke his exploits – and harness the power of the biting winds that sweep over the plateau.*

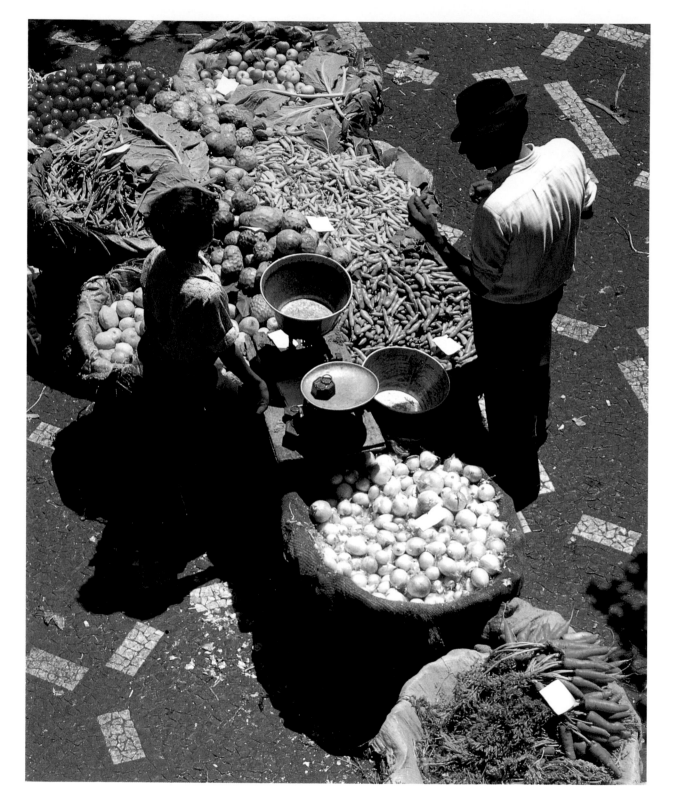

PAELLA VALENCIANA

RICE WITH CHICKEN AND SEAFOOD

The most famous rice dish in the world, my recipe is adapted from the one José Ramos, chef at La Fonda in Marbella, makes in his own garden.

SERVES 6 – 8

*1 kg (2 lb) chicken with giblets, or 3 small chicken
legs plus a chicken carcass*
*700 g (1½ lb) monkfish on the bone, or 500 g (1 lb)
white fish fillets, plus some fish bones*
250 g (8 oz) prawns in the shell
500 g (1 lb) clams or mussels, cleaned (see page 96)
250 g (8 oz) baby squid, cleaned (see page 95)
*500 g (1 lb 2 oz) Spanish medium-grain, or risotto,
rice, washed*
500 g (1 lb) onions, chopped
*tender pods from 300 g (10 oz) podded peas, or 1
celery stalk, chopped, plus 50 g (2 oz) mange-tout,
trimmed, in short lengths*
400 g (14 oz) canned tomatoes, with juice
250 g (8 oz) green peppers, seeded and cut in squares
100 g (4 oz) French beans, trimmed, in short lengths
*75 g (3 oz) cooked chickpeas or haricot beans, or
frozen broad beans*
75 g (3 oz) peas
5 fat garlic cloves, finely chopped
about 150 ml (¼ pt) olive oil
150 ml (¼ pt) white wine
1 bay leaf
20 saffron strands or 2 × 2 g packets of powder
2 teaspoons paprika
salt and freshly ground black pepper

Start by making a good stock. Strip the flesh off the chicken and cut into large chunks. Joint the legs, then halve, chopping through the bone with a heavy knife. Put the carcass (and giblets) into a stockpot.

Cut the fish into chunks about 5 cm (2 in) wide and remove any skin. Reserving 6 whole prawns for decoration, shell the prawns, putting the shells and fish debris in the stockpot. Add 1 chopped onion, half the

FRUIT AND VEGETABLE MARKET *Whatever is fresh and locally available can be gathered up and used in a* paella.

pea pods, or celery stalk, and the bay leaf and cover with water. Simmer for an hour then strain. Measure the liquid, add the wine and reduce again until you have about 1.2 l (2 pt) liquid. Pour a little over the saffron in a cup and keep the rest ready in a saucepan.

Prepare the shellfish. Heat some of the stock in another saucepan and add half the clams or mussels. When they open, remove them and discard the shells. Cut the squid bodies into rings and keep the tentacles in a bunch. Check through the recipe and prepare all the ingredients, grouping things that are added together. Drain the tomato juice into the main stock and cut the tomatoes into strips. The recipe takes an hour from this point.

Use a *paella* pan about 40 cm (15½ in) across or a wide shallow casserole which will hold 4 l (7 pt). Heat 4 tablespoons of oil over gentle heat and soften the onions. Season the chicken pieces, increase the heat, and fry the chicken until golden. Add the peppers and the remaining pods or mange-tout and stir-fry for about 5 minutes – more oil may be needed. Season well.

Add a little more oil, then toss the squid tentacles in it, so they stiffen. Reserve these for the garnish. Season the fish pieces and add them to the pan. (If you are not using a *paella* pan it is easier to do this in a separate frying pan, with more oil.) Fry them on both sides and then add the squid rings.

Fry the garlic and add the rice to the main pan. Stir the rice in the oil and let it fry for 3–4 minutes, sprinkling it with paprika. (If the fish was fried separately, fit it in now.) Add a third of the hot stock to the pan, all the beans and peas with the shelled prawns and shelled clams or mussels. Stir the rice for the last time, making sure everything is evenly distributed, then tuck in the unshelled clams or mussels.

Arrange the tomato strips across the surface and pour in another third of the hot liquid. Reduce the heat to the minimum and start to shift the pan regularly, if the heat source is smaller than the pan bottom. (A thin pan, or a deep one, is best cooked in the oven at 180° C [350° F, gas 4] from this point.)

Add the remaining stock and continue cooking for 15–20 minutes. Test a rice grain: if it's cooked, decorate the top with the unshelled prawns and squid tentacles. Cover the top – traditionally it is wrapped in layers of newspaper – and let it sit for 10 minutes for the rice to absorb the final liquid. In Spain, red wine is served with *paella* – try Faustino V *reserva*.

PAELLA DE VERDURAS DEL TIEMPO

PAELLA OF SPRING VEGETABLES

A *paella* can contain many things through the changing seasons – bacon, chard, tomatoes, white or black beans and turnips – usually with some part of the pig. Here is a pretty dish with the new season's vegetables. Fresh broad beans can be substituted for the asparagus, and chopped mushroom for the ham.

SERVES 6

400 g (14 oz) Spanish medium-grain, or risotto, rice, washed
850 ml (1½ pt) good stock
150 ml (¼ pt) dry white wine
200 g (7 oz) trimmed asparagus tips, in short lengths
1 small onion, chopped
2 garlic cloves, finely chopped
175 g (6 oz) raw gammon or bacon, chopped small
200 g (7 oz) green beans, trimmed, in short lengths
2 small courgettes, thinly sliced
1 carrot, diced
1 tomato, without skin or seeds, diced
100 g (4 oz) mange-tout, trimmed, snapped in half
4 tablespoons olive oil
4 tablespoons chopped parsley
salt and freshly ground black pepper

Heat the oil in a *paella* pan or wide shallow casserole and fry the onion gently with the gammon or bacon. When nearly soft, add the garlic. Add 2 tablespoons of parsley and the rice, stirring it in the oil for a minute or so.

Combine the stock and wine and taste it, adding seasoning as needed. If it is tasteless, boil to concentrate it, adding wine to make up the volume. Add a third to the rice, bring to simmering point and add the asparagus. The rice takes 20–25 minutes from the moment the first batch of stock is added.

When the stock has been absorbed, add another third, with the beans, courgettes, carrot and tomato, and stir for the last time. Add the remaining stock with the mange-tout. When the rice is done, cover the pan and let it stand, off the heat, for 5 minutes, then garnish with more parsley. This is good served with slices of fried ham.

ARROZ A BANDA

FRAGRANT RICE FOLLOWED BY FISH AND ALIOLI

A banda means 'apart' in the Valencian dialect, and in this recipe from the Alicante coast the rice is served first – without the fish that gives the stock in which it is cooked so much flavour. The fish then follows, hot, barely warm or cold, accompanied by a rich golden *alioli*. Different towns on the coast feature different fish for the second dish – at Catarroja, south of Valencia, it is grey mullet, for example. But it is generally agreed that rascasse and scorpion fish make the best base for the stock. I use a conger eel head or plaice skin and bones for stock, red mullet for colour, a firm white fish like monkfish and a more delicately flavoured one like hake. Ask the fishmonger to clean, descale and fillet the fish but take home the heads and bones.

SERVES 6

2.5 kg (5 lb) whole fish, 3–4 kinds, calculating one-third of the weight for fillets, and the rest for stock
100 g (4 oz) tiny shrimps (optional)
12–18 new potatoes (250–350 g [8–12 oz])
2 onions, chopped
2 garlic cloves, finely chopped
200 g (7 oz) canned tomatoes, with juice
1 green pepper, seeded and chopped
2 bay leaves
10 black peppercorns, crushed
parsley stalks plus 4 tablespoons finely chopped leaves
125 ml (4 fl oz) dry white wine

FRAGRANT RICE
700 ml (1 pt 4 fl oz) stock from the fish bones
250 ml (8 fl oz) dry white wine
400 g (14 oz) Spanish medium-grain, or risotto, rice, washed
4 garlic cloves, finely chopped
10 saffron strands or 2 g packet powder
3 tablespoons olive oil

EGG-YOLK ALIOLI
6 cloves of garlic, finely chopped
¼ teaspoon salt
2 egg yolks
200 ml (7 fl oz) virgin olive oil

First make the stock. Rinse the fish heads and bones, put them in a stockpot with the onion, garlic, tomato, green pepper, bay leaves, crushed peppercorns and the stalks from the parsley, snapped in several places. Cover with about 1.5 l (3 pt) water. Cook for 45 minutes from the time it starts simmering. Strain the stock; you will need about 1 l (1¾ pt) for cooking the fish. Put the saffron in a cup and pour a little stock over it.

Make the *alioli*. Crush the garlic and salt to a paste in a mortar, or with the flat of a knife on a hard board then move to a bowl. Add the egg yolks and whisk hard, adding the oil, a little at a time as for mayonnaise. This makes a thick butter (which can be thinned with 2 tablespoons of very strong, reduced fish stock).

Heat the stock with the saffron liquid and 250 ml (8 fl oz) wine and add the potatoes, and shrimps, if using. Cook for 5 minutes, then add the fish fillets. Simmer gently, covered, for 10 minutes.

Start the fragrant rice. Heat 2 tablespoons of oil in a *paella* pan or shallow casserole and fry the garlic, then the rice. Stir-fry for 3–4 minutes.

When the fish is ready, remove the fish fillets, potatoes and shellfish, to a big shallow dish, and cover with foil. Strain the fish stock through a sieve (there should be 1 l [1¾ pt]) and reserve 150 ml (¼ pt) in a saucepan for reheating the fish. Pour half of the main stock on to the rice and stir. After 10 minutes add the remaining stock and cook for another 10–12 minutes. The liquid should all be absorbed. When the rice is done, turn off the heat, cover and let it stand for 10 minutes. Serve the rice as it is or, at the most, garnished with a few soup shrimps.

To reheat the fish and potatoes, bring the reserved stock to the boil with 125 ml (4 fl oz) of white wine and pour over the fillets. Put in the oven at 180° C (350° F, gas 4) for 10 minutes, then decorate with a little parsley. Serve this as the second course, accompanied by the *alioli*.

Fine-flavoured rice, without any distractions, can take a good *manzanilla* sherry. Partner it with a glass of cold water and something special from an *almacenista* – a maturer of wines who buys from small producers: Emilio Lustau ships such wines abroad.

After this, serve something a little refreshing with the fish: like a fruity white Rioja Navajas *blanco crianza*, made with 100% Viura, the Spanish white wine grape, or CUNE's Monopole.

SELLING GARLIC AND ONIONS *An improvized hat provides extra protection from the sun.*

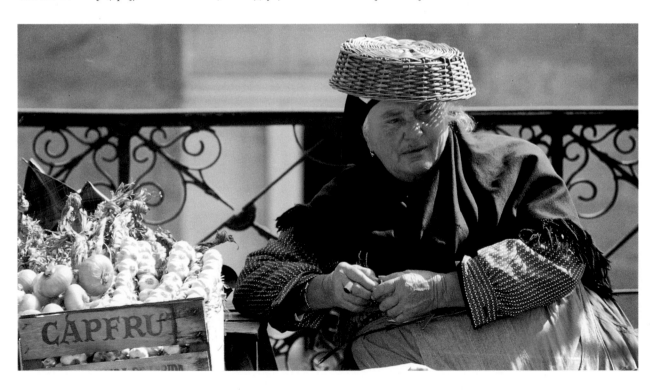

ARROZ CON COSTRA AL ESTILO DE ELCHE

RICE WITH A CRISP EGG CRUST

Unusually, this *paella* is baked in the oven and has a rich golden crust over the top, which is broken to release the fragrance of the rice and all the meats hidden in it – the 'hidden treasures', as they have been called.

It's a good dish for the end of Christmas, as it can incorporate stuffing balls, a variety of different leftover meats and turkey stock. The recipe is given here, however, with freshly cooked meats, so you can judge the quantities.

SERVES 4 – 5

500 g (1 lb) Spanish medium-grain, or risotto, rice, washed

1 onion, chopped

2 garlic cloves, finely chopped

250 g (8 oz) ripe tomatoes, without skin or seeds, or 200 g (7 oz) canned tomatoes with juice

150 g (5 oz) dried chickpeas, soaked in boiling water for 1 hour (see page 11)

6 large eggs

1½ – 2½ l (2½ – 4¼ pt) stock

2 g packet saffron powder

1 dried chilli, seeded and chopped

salt and freshly ground black pepper

50 ml (2 fl oz) olive oil

'HIDDEN TREASURES'

½ chicken or 3 chicken legs

100 g (4 oz) smoked gammon or bacon in one piece

200 g (7 oz) cooking chorizo, morcilla or black pudding, or other fresh spicy sausage

250 g (8 oz) lean veal or pork, minced

250 g (8 oz) lean pork, cubed

2 good pinches of ground cumin

¼ teaspoon ground cinnamon

flour

Drain the chickpeas and cover generously with stock or water. Bring to the boil and simmer for ½ hour. When they start to soften, begin to make the 'hidden treasures'. Add the chicken, bacon and sausages to the chickpeas with the dried chilli and simmer for a further ½ hour, when the chickpeas should be cooked. Remove the meats, leave to cool a little and cut into bite-sized chunks, discarding bones and skin.

Meanwhile flavour the minced veal well with salt, cumin and cinnamon and roll into large marble-sized balls. Beat the eggs together, coat the meat balls lightly, then reserve the eggs for the crust. Then move the balls to a plate covered with plenty of flour and shake it to and fro until the balls are coated.

In a wide shallow casserole that will hold 4 l (7 pt), heat the oil and fry the veal balls over a high heat, shaking frequently so they colour and crisp on all sides. Remove from the pan. Season the pork cubes and fry until well coloured; reserve with the meat balls.

Next, make the flavouring for the rice. Soften the chopped onion in the pan, then add the garlic. Next, add the chopped tomato flesh, season and let it reduce to a sauce. The recipe can be cooked in advance up to this point.

Heat the oven to 170° C (325° F, gas 3). Add the rice to the hot tomato sauce and stir for a minute or two. Drain the chickpeas and make up the cooking liquid with stock to 1.5 l (2½ pt). Bring this to the boil, adding the saffron powder, and taste it. This is the moment to add white wine (reducing the liquid again), paprika, even a stock cube, if the liquid is characterless, for this is the flavour the rice will assume presently.

Pour the stock into the rice and tomato mixture and bring slowly to the boil, stirring occasionally. Cook the rice for 10 minutes. Add the chickpeas and all the prepared meats, distributing them round the pan. Bring back to the boil. Move the pan to the oven and cook for a further 15 minutes.

Then whisk the eggs with a little salt and a tablespoon of water. Pour this over the rice, covering the whole surface. Turn up the oven to its highest heat and return the pan for 10 minutes. The dish should then rest, with the oven turned off and the door open, for about 10 minutes before serving. As there is such a medley of flavours in the dish, drink something simple like a good supermarket's own label red Rioja.

APARTMENT BLOCK *The infinitely varied greens of these wicker blinds add to the sense of rich and busy lives going on behind them.*

ARROZ CON JEREZ

RICE WITH SHERRY

A rich, medium dry sherry gives this rice an intriguing southern accent – ideal to accompany a roast pork loin or tenderloin, cooked with a little garlic and a generous glass of the same sherry.

Another good side dish is made with all stock and the addition of 2 tablespoons each of toasted pine-nuts and chopped almonds at the end.

SERVES 4

400 g (14 oz) Spanish medium-grain, or risotto, rice, washed
225 ml (8 fl oz) amontillado sherry
2 tablespoons olive oil
1 onion, chopped
2 garlic cloves, finely chopped
1 l (1¾ pt) good chicken stock, hot
salt and freshly ground black pepper
pinch of cayenne pepper

Heat the oil in a *paella* pan or wide shallow casserole and fry the onion until soft and golden, adding the garlic near the end. Add the rice and turn in the oil for a minute or so. Add most of the sherry and let it bubble.

Sample the stock, adding salt and pepper as needed, so that the seasoning is very lively. Add to the rice, bring to simmering point then turn down the heat. Cook for 20 minutes without stirring. Turn off the heat, sprinkle with the remaining sherry and cover with a lid. Let the rice steam gently for 10 minutes to absorb the last drops of liquid.

FIDEUA DE MARISCOS

PASTA WITH SEAFOOD

Somehow pasta has taken over from rice in this seafood dish from the Costa Brava, which is made in a *paella* pan. Combine these shellfish with rice, and the dish becomes a *paella de mariscos*. The recipe is made from whatever shellfish are available in the market.

This is by far the easiest – and cheapest – of the big, bravura shellfish dishes. The quantity can be multiplied three or four times for a party, as it can be cooked successfully in a deeper pan – unlike *paella*.

The traditional pasta of Catalonia is *fideos* – only about 2.5 cm (1 in) long and the thickness of fine spaghetti. However, I look for a pasta needing 8–10 minutes' cooking, for this is the ideal time to let the shellfish flavours blend into the stock and then into the pasta itself.

SERVES 4

4 langoustines (Dublin Bay prawns with their heads), or big prawns
100 g (4 oz) peeled prawns, or 250 g (8 oz) shrimps
300 g (10 oz) hake, cubed
175 g (6 oz) small squid, cleaned and sliced (see page 95)
250 g (8 oz) clams or small mussels, cleaned (see page 96)
400 g (14 oz) fine spaghetti, broken in short lengths
1 onion, finely chopped
2 garlic cloves, finely chopped
100 g (4 oz) ripe tomato, without skin or seeds
750 ml (1¼ pt) good fish stock (see page 16)
250 ml (8 fl oz) dry white wine
2 tablespoons olive oil
pinch of cayenne pepper or ½ dried chilli, seeded
1 bay leaf
lemon wedges to garnish (optional)

Heat the oil in a shallow casserole and fry the onion gently until soft, adding the garlic towards the end. Put in the tomato with the cayenne or chilli and bay leaf, stirring occasionally until soft and reduced.

Add the stock and wine and bring to the boil. Add the pasta, hake cubes and Dublin Bay prawns and cook for 5 minutes. Add the squid and other shellfish and cook for another 5 minutes or until the pasta is done and all the liquid absorbed. *Alioli* (see page 54) is sometimes stirred in at the end or accompanies it.

The rich buttery-tasting Chardonnay grapes are part of a new-style wine-making in Catalonia, and make whites that will stand up to all the different flavours of this dish. Look for Raimat Chardonnay from Lérida or the slightly pineapply Torres Gran Viña Sol, with about half Chardonnay grapes.

CANELONES
CON LANGOSTINOS

FRIED CANNELLONI WITH PRAWNS

Cannelloni are a popular part of Spanish cuisine and are eaten all over the country with a variety of fillings. These unusual cannelloni from the Costa Brava are crisp on the outside and the meltingly creamy middle has a real taste of the sea. They consist almost entirely of delicious fat prawns, just held together by a little sauce and the cannelloni, then deep-fried.

A hot starter that can be made almost entirely in advance, the dish also makes a good late-night supper for two or three.

SERVES 4

8 cannelloni, plus a few spares
700 g (1½ lb) prawns in the shell, or
250 g (8 oz) peeled prawns
50 ml (2 fl oz) dry Martini (or ¼ chicken stock cube,
plus a little paprika and nutmeg)
1 bay leaf (optional)

150 – 200 ml (5 – 7 fl oz) milk
2 tablespoons flour
2 tablespoons melted butter
1 large egg
salt and freshly ground black pepper

BEER BATTER
1 large egg
2 tablespoons butter
100 g (4 oz) flour
125 – 150 ml (4 – 5 fl oz) beer (lager or pale ale)
a little freshly grated nutmeg
olive oil for deep frying

If you have prawns in the shell, peel them, putting the heads and shells into a pan with the Martini and bay leaf. Add water almost to cover and simmer very gently for 30 minutes. Strain the stock, return to the pan and boil to reduce to about 4 tablespoons. Add milk to bring up to 200 ml (7 fl oz) and warm it. If using peeled prawns, warm the larger quantity of milk with the stock cube and flavour carefully with a little paprika and nutmeg.

Melt 2 tablespoons of butter in a small pan and stir in 2 tablespoons of flour. Cook for a minute, then stir in the milk. Bring to the boil slowly, stirring, and cook for a minute or so. Take off the heat, beat in an egg and leave until cold.

Bring some water to the boil in a small roasting tin and put in 8 cannelloni (plus 2 – 3 spares if using Italian quick-cook cannelloni, as these tend to split). Cook for 8 minutes, shaking the pan occasionally to make sure they are not sticking, then drain carefully.

Chop the peeled prawns coarsely, mix with the white sauce – just enough to make the prawns adhere – and stuff 8 cannelloni. Chill well.

About 15 mintues before serving, make the batter. Beat the egg and melted butter into the flour. Gradually beat in the beer to make a smooth batter and season with nutmeg, pepper and salt. Heat the oil, at least 4 cm (1½ – 2 in) deep, in a wide casserole. Dip the stuffed cannelloni, one at a time on a fish slice, into the batter. Slide into the oil, allowing 10 seconds between each one, as they are cold and the oil must reheat. When 4 are frying in a row, turn them over gently with a slotted spoon. When golden on both sides, lift them out in the original order and drain on kitchen paper. Fry the second batch and serve promptly. A delicate young white wine, like the local Marqués de Alella, which is slightly spritzy, makes a good partner.

Verduras y Ensaladas

VEGETABLES AND SALADS

All the sun-drenched colours and richness of Spain seem to have been absorbed by the country's vegetables and the simple but exuberant dishes they produce.

ENSALADA DE NARANJAS VALENCIANAS *left (p 74)*,
TOMATES RELLENOS A LA ALICANTINA *right (p 71)*.

THE WONDERFUL IMMEDIACY OF SPANISH food is seen at its best in Spanish vegetables, which reach the plate in the shortest possible time. Think of the popular salad *ensalada mixta*, with great chunks of sunny tomato, lettuce just hours from the field, pungent, juicy onion rings and a scattering of olives. The dressing is left to you: simple and satisfying!

The colours of the vegetables, their freshness and generous size, make market shopping in Spain an extraordinary pleasure. Huge bunches of chard, for example, with glossy dark leaves and pearl-white stalks, the size of a small wheat-sheaf, bright red heaps of peppers, crates of lettuce, bales of bay leaves – everything comes in generous quantities but at small cost. No wonder Spain has become the market garden of Europe.

Every vegetable is valued. It's not a side show to the main dish, but a separate course, on its own plate. The vocabulary reflects this attention: where English only has 'bean' for example, there are 14 or more Spanish words, distinguishing the different types. There are two nouns for sweet potatoes, according to the colour inside. Cabbage is *col*, *berza*, *repollo* or *lombarda* according to its shape and colour. There are also a host of regional words, which reflect the local feeling that just there, in that corner of Spain, grow the best peas, or artichokes, or beans in the world.

Vegetables are seasonal, which adds to their pleasure. The range is local but may include rarities unobtainable elsewhere, like the cardoon, cousin of the artichoke, whose stalks are eaten on Christmas Eve. There are also wild foods like spring asparagus and palmetto hearts, cut from small palms at Easter. *Tagarnina* is a thistle popular in *tortillas* in winter in the south. Fat capers, *alcaparras*, grow on the mountains behind the south and east coasts, and make ideal partners for fried fish like *mero*, grouper, and shark.

At the base of the vegetable pot there are often chickpeas. *Garbanzos* were introduced to Spain by the Carthaginians and the Roman writer, Plautus, ridiculed the chickpea-eating Spaniards, just as Shakespeare mocked the Welsh for eating toasted cheese. This curious dried pea, shaped 'like a widow's nose and a dressmaker's backside', is attractively chewy, and fairs also sell them as a snack, ready-cooked and salted.

But the 'meat of Spain' is the olive. Looking out from the beautiful Giralda tower of what was once the Seville mosque, there is a sea of olive trees, as far as the eye can see, in the flat Guadalquivir valley. The Arabs did not introduce the tree, but they planted them more widely and spread the taste for olive oil, one of the basic flavours of Spanish cooking.

The Moors ruled over at least a part of Spain for almost 1000 years. 'A land which hovers between Europe and Africa, between the hat and the turban,' Richard Ford called it in *Gatherings from Spain* in 1846. The Moors introduced rice and irrigated the south, planting citrus fruits and almonds, and starting the system that now supports the green beans and the mint, the melons, tomatoes and the garlic.

They also brought new vegetables, like aubergines, from the East and in the kitchen their legacy is very visible, in the many words that have the prefix *al*. *Almuerzo, albóndigas, almíbar, almirez* – lunch, meatballs, sugar syrup and the brass mortar – are but a few. The mortar and pestle has became a basic adjunct to soup-and-sauce-making, crushing fried bread, toasted almonds and garlic cloves. 'That gay prelude to an Andalusian meal', Gerald Brenan called the noise of pounding. With their thoughtfulness about spicing and textures, the introduction of cumin and cinnamon, the fondness for saffron, and an understanding of sweet and savoury, the Moors made Spain the European centre of civilized cooking.

The second great wave of change in Spain was the introduction of vegetables from America. John Gerrard's *Herbal*, in 1597, remarks in wonder on Spanish tomatoes. With them came peppers and chillies, at first regarded only as a flavouring for tomatoes. Spanish cooks now choose judiciously between the different types of capsicum needed for a dish, as the British might specify a particular lettuce.

The potato, too, found its first European home near Seville, where the account books of the local nuns for 1576 record their purchase. The many varieties of kidney beans were each adopted in different parts of Spain, augmenting the tough local broad bean. These new vegetables transformed the Spanish diet and vegetables throughout Europe were never to be the same again.

COLIFLOR AL ESTILO DE BADAJOZ

FRIED CAULIFLOWER

Simple and surprisingly tasty – as food from poor regions like Extremadura often is – this is also a good way to use up leftover cauliflower.

SERVES 4

1 large cauliflower
1 garlic clove, finely chopped
2 tablespoons finely chopped parsley
2 large eggs, beaten
¼ teaspoon salt
freshly ground black pepper
6 tablespoons wine vinegar
flour for coating
olive oil for frying

Separate the cauliflower into florets, trimming back the smaller stems and splitting any larger bunches. Cook them for 5 minutes in a generous quantity of boiling salted water, then drain well.

Mash the garlic to a paste with the salt, using the flat side of a knife or a pestle and mortar. Mix the vinegar into the paste and pour over the cauliflower in a wide bowl. Sprinkle with pepper and parsley and leave to marinate for 30 minutes, turning the cauliflower once.

Turn the florets in flour on a plate, then dip in beaten egg. Fry in hot oil, turning them over until golden on all sides. If there is parsley left in the marinade bowl, this can be sprinkled on top. The cauliflower may also be served with a tomato sauce.

PIMIENTOS CON NATA

GRILLED RED PEPPERS WITH CREAM

Aragon is known for its peppers: long, pointed, spicy *pimientos de piquillo*, and this is the ingredient I most regret not being able to buy outside Spain. This simple dish is surprisingly effective, even when made with bell peppers. It comes from the hilltop town of Sos del Rey Católico, famous as the birthplace of Ferdinand of Aragon, who united Spain by marrying Isabella of Castile in 1474.

SERVES 6

6 red peppers
175 ml (6 fl oz) whipping cream
pinch of caster sugar
pinch of salt

Grill the peppers for about 20 minutes, giving them a quarter turn every 5 minutes, until they are charred on all sides. Put them in a plastic bag for 10 minutes, then strip off the charred skins and pull out and discard the stalks and seeds. Do this on a plate to catch all the sweet juices from the peppers.

Trim off the top and bottom of each pepper and open them to remove the last seeds. Purée the trimmings and juices in a blender.

Arrange the peppers on a serving plate, or preferably individual dishes, and reheat in a low oven or under a low grill. Heat the cream, stir in the purée, plus the sugar and salt, then pour it over the peppers and serve immediately.

CALÇOTS AMB ROMESCO

GRILLED SPRING ONIONS
WITH ROMESCO SAUCE

I was about to leave out the recipe for these most delicious of barbecue vegetables when I realized that every Chinese store sells the fat spring onions that it needs. In Valls, in the province of Tarragona, the coming of spring and warmer weather is marked by *la calçotada*, a party out in the fields to pick this special, juicy onion.

Toasted on a barbecue, until black on the outside, and eaten with swordfish, lightly dressed with sherry vinegar, or arranged between trout under a grill, they make a wonderful fish accompaniment. In season, however, they are a dish by themselves with a traditional sauce. Bibs are often provided as removing the outside can be a messy business.

The onions are produced by plucking out every central sprouting shoot from onions in store, at the end of the year. The shoots are then planted, watered once and picked a couple of months later.

SERVES 4

*12 – 16 big spring onions, about 2.5 cm (1 in) in
diameter, or the fattest you can buy
1 tablespoon melted butter
1 tablespoon olive oil
romesco sauce (see page 88)*

Cut off the soft green tips and brush the onions with the mixed butter and oil. Grill for 15 minutes, turning once, until black on the outside. Everyone peels their own, so provide plenty of napkins. Serve with *romesco*, the piquant chilli-flavoured sauce.

MOUNTAIN FARM *The rich variations of the Spanish climate and landscape, encompassing stark, arid plains and lush, green hills, are one factor behind its extraordinarily diverse cuisine.*

ACELGAS CON PASAS
Y PIÑONES

SPINACH WITH RAISINS
AND PINE-NUTS

This is a popular dish round the Mediterranean, and nowadays it is commonly made, as here, with the leaves of chard or with spinach, which is easier to find. However I have an old Malagueñan recipe, which uses the white chard ribs only, cut into 5 cm (2 in) lengths, with the local fat raisins.

SERVES 4

*1 kg (2 lb) spinach or chard, more if stalks are big
4 tablespoons raisins (seedless muscatels are best)
3 tablespoons pine-nuts
2 tablespoons olive oil
1 onion, finely chopped
1 garlic clove, finely chopped
salt and freshly ground black pepper
4 tostadas – slices of toast or fried bread*

Soak the raisins in boiling water to plump them. Heat the oil and fry the pine-nuts, turning them constantly until golden. Remove and add the onion. Fry the onion until golden then add the garlic.

Wash the spinach or chard, stripping out the stems. Cook spinach in only the water clinging to the leaves, in a covered pan, turning the top to the bottom occasionally – it takes about 10 minutes. Chard is tougher – cook in boiling water for 15 minutes. Drain and chop.

Stir the chopped leaves into the onion, adding the drained raisins and nuts; season and heat through. Serve with *tostadas*.

ROVELLONS AL AJILLO

WILD MUSHROOMS WITH GARLIC

In September in Catalonia and the Basque country, serious-looking men swarm into the mountains to pick mushrooms. *Rovellon* is the Catalan name for Spain's best-loved mushroom, called *níscalo* in Castilian – a stunning golden yellow underneath. Big ones become cup-shaped, like communion chalices, pleated on the underside. A true *rovellon* will 'bleed' from the stem when cut – single drops of blood-like juice reminiscent of a medieval miracle – and this gives them their English name of 'bleeding milk cap'.

The Spaniards would certainly allow 250 g (8 oz) a head, but if you can find wild mushrooms like chanterelles, 175 g (6 oz) is enough for two. Don't over-cook or over-chop wild things, but treat them gently and let them show off their natural fragrance of the woods. Brown mushrooms are the best cultivated substitute available.

An old-fashioned starter for four served with, or on, fried bread, accompany it with chilled *palo cortado*, a medium dry sherry, in sweetness between an *amontillado* and an *oloroso*. The dish also makes a delicious supper for two.

SERVES 2

250 g (8 oz) brown mushrooms (sold in supermarkets as chestnut, hazelnut, marron or brown cap mushrooms)
1 tablespoon butter
1 tablespoon olive oil
1 small garlic clove, finely chopped
salt and freshly ground black pepper
1 tablespoon finely chopped parsley

Heat the butter and oil in a frying pan and add the chopped garlic and sliced mushrooms. Fry them quickly – they are very meaty and don't lose their shape or make juice in the pan. Turn the mushrooms over occasionally with a wooden spoon. Season and sprinkle them with parsley.

HABAS RONDEÑAS

BROAD BEANS WITH HAM, RONDA STYLE

Ronda, in Andalusia, is famous throughout Spain as the place where Francisco Romero laid down the rules of bullfighting in the 18th century, and nothing is too good for fighting bulls, who are fed for the contest on broad beans. Broad beans also combine particularly well with *serrano*, the local raw ham. Now that tender frozen beans are available in every supermarket this is almost a storecupboard dish.

SERVES 6

1 kg (2 lb) frozen broad beans
175 g (6 oz) raw ham, smoked gammon or back bacon
4 tablespoons olive oil
175 g (6 oz) mild Spanish onion, chopped
1 garlic clove, finely chopped
4 large eggs
salt and freshly ground black pepper
50 g (2 oz) parsley sprigs, chopped

Dice the ham (or cut the bacon into strips). Heat the oil in a flameproof casserole and add the onion and ham or bacon. Fry very gently until the bacon has given off its fat and the onion is soft. Add the garlic towards the end.

Stir in the frozen beans, cover, turn down the heat and cook until tender, stirring occasionally – this should take about 12 minutes.

Meanwhile hard boil the eggs for 10 minutes and chop them. Season the beans generously, stir in the chopped eggs and heat through. Stir in the parsley. In summer, when parsley is almost unobtainable in the south of Spain, diced red pepper or tomato may be used instead to garnish the dish.

VINES IN LA MANCHA *Low-growing vines cover much of La Mancha, Spain's largest single wine-producing area.*

LA RIOJA ALTA (overleaf) *The higher part of the Rioja area, the Rioja Alta, has a cooler, wetter climate and a soil which yields the acidity necessary to produce its distinctive wines.*

MENESTRA A LA BILBAINA

BILBAO MIXED VEGETABLE POT

A dish celebrating the new vegetables of spring, *menestra* is made all along the northern coast of Spain, as far as the French Basque country, where it is called *coussinat*. The ingredients are measured in handfuls: whatever is available is gathered up and put to use.

A seemingly simple dish, it can achieve considerable sophistication in the hands of a good cook. In Asturias fried potatoes and ham are added at the end, while in Navarre the artichoke bases, and lengths of chard stalk, are floured and fried for contrasting texture.

SERVES 6

100 g (4 oz) ham or gammon, diced
2 tablespoons diced ham fat or olive oil
the trimmed bases of 4 artichokes (see page 103)
1 onion, chopped
3 garlic cloves, finely chopped
250 g (8 oz) podded peas, reserving a few tender pods
250 g (8 oz) green beans, trimmed, in short lengths
250 g (8 oz) podded broad beans
250 g (8 oz) young carrots, in short lengths
6 tablespoons chopped parsley
175 ml (6 fl oz) dry white wine
300 ml (½ pt) light meat or chicken stock
2 hard-boiled eggs, chopped
salt and freshly ground black pepper

Heat the ham fat or oil in a casserole and soften the onion, adding the garlic and 2 tablespoons of parsley towards the end. Remove the onion to a blender and reduce to a purée with a little of the wine. Add the diced ham to the casserole and fry gently.

Bring a saucepan of salted water to the boil and add the stock to the casserole and bring to the boil. Then cook the vegetables in the following sequence. Add the broad beans to the casserole, at the same time putting the peas (plus a few tender pods) into the simmering water. After 10 minutes add the quartered artichoke bases to the casserole and the remaining vegetables to the simmering water, and cook for 10 minutes.

Drain the boiled vegetables and add them to the casserole. Add the wine and the onion purée, warming the liquid and turning the vegetables gently. Check the seasoning and serve in soup plates with a little of the juices, sprinkled with chopped egg and parsley.

JUDÍAS BLANCAS A LO TÍO LUCAS

UNCLE LUKE'S MILDLY SPICED BEANS

Behind this warming dish of spicy beans stands the comfortable figure of a barkeeper called Uncle Luke. He invented it in the early years of the 19th century for the poor sailors who frequented Cadiz, living on credit while they waited to be paid off at the end of each voyage. Uncle Luke then moved to Madrid, where he opened a hostelry, and here his excellent beans achieved national fame.

SERVES 6

500 g (1 lb) dried haricot beans
150 g (5 oz) thick, fat bacon or a gammon chop
2 tablespoon olive oil
2 large onions, chopped
1 garlic bulb, cloves peeled and finely chopped
2 tablespoons tomato paste
1 bay leaf
2 teaspoons paprika
1 tablespoon vinegar
¼ teaspoon ground cumin
pinch of ground cloves
1 tablespoon finely chopped parsley
¼ teaspoon ground white pepper
1 teaspoon salt

Soak the beans for 1 hour in boiling water, or overnight in plenty of cold water.

Cut the fat off the bacon or gammon chop and fry the onion and chopped bacon fat in the olive oil in the bottom of a bean pot or casserole. After 10 minutes add the lean meat, chopped to the size of small soup croûtons, then the garlic. Drain the beans and add them to the pot with the remaining ingredients and enough water to cover them well.

Simmer for $1\frac{1}{4}$ – $1\frac{1}{2}$ hours, until the beans are soft, checking occasionally that they are not catching or drying out. There should be enough liquid to give each person a couple of spoonfuls with the beans. Check the seasonings and serve as a starter in soup plates. The beans also make a good side dish with fatty meat like streaky bacon and sausages, or roast shoulder of lamb.

MIGAS DE PASTOR

CRISP FRIED BREADCRUMBS

Bread plays a large part in the Spanish diet, and very good bread it is, crisp and fresh. Better, the Spaniards would say, than French bread, which is the perfect substitute. Not so long ago in country places a kilo a day (about 2 lb) was a common portion, as an accompaniment to vegetables or meat, and a mopper-up of sauces.

Bread is never eaten stale. Such value is placed on it that dressers in old country kitchens have a special drawer for yesterday's bread, which is then used for cooking. Crumbs thicken sauces, slices lie at the bottom of soup plates and *tostadas* may accompany vegetables – try them fried in the red fat from *manteca colorada* (see page 28). Though Spanish bread is white, a brown loaf is the better choice if the only alternative is the sliced white packet variety.

These savoury crumbs are eaten all over Spain, though particularly associated with Aragon. In poor places like Extremadura they are used to eke out cooked vegetables – or accompany eggs and bacon. Gerald Brenan's landlord ate them with sardines and chocolate sauce – together! This recipe came originally from the Military Academy at Zaragoza.

SERVES 4

4 thick slices of bread, cut from a loaf, stale enough to be firm
2 garlic cloves, bruised with the flat of a knife
oil for frying
salt and freshly ground black pepper
pisto (see page 50) or samfaina (see page 88) (optional)

Cut off the crusts and cut the bread into 1 cm ($\frac{1}{2}$ in) cubes. Sprinkle with water, season with salt and pepper and wrap up overnight in a napkin.

Half an hour before serving, heat the oil with the garlic cloves. When it smokes, discard the garlic and add the crumbs. Cook them for 12–15 minutes, moving them constantly.

Serve the breadcrumbs very hot, as a partner to a tomato stew – they are also frequently served with bacon and eggs.

TOMATES RELLENOS A LA ALICANTINA

STUFFED TOMATOES FROM ALICANTE

A simple stuffed tomato dish, with spinach, orange juice and nuts, from the east coast.

SERVES 4

4 large ripe tomatoes, over 250 g (8 oz) each
500 g (1 lb) spinach
150 – 200 g (6 – 7 oz) raw ham, gammon or back bacon
4 – 5 tablespoons butter
1 tablespoon olive oil (if using ham)
grated zest and juice 1 orange
salt and freshly ground black pepper
50 g (2 oz) blanched almonds

Wash and drain the spinach, stripping out the stalks. Wash again, tearing up bigger leaves. Put 2 tablespoons of butter into a large pan and cook the spinach in the water clinging to the leaves, with the lid on. After 5 minutes, remove the lid, turn the top leaves to the bottom and cook for 10 minutes more, uncovered.

Meanwhile, heat the oven to 180° C (350° F, gas 4). Halve the tomatoes across and scoop out the insides with a spoon. Arrange the halves in a large greased dish. If you are using raw ham, put 1 tablespoon each of butter and olive oil into a saucepan, heat and add the chopped ham. If you are using gammon or bacon, cut off and dice the fat; add 2 tablespoons of fat cubes to the pan. Heat until the fat runs, then add the cubed lean meat. Drain the spinach and chop it well – a board with a groove around is useful to prevent the juices making a mess. Add to the pan, turning it in the fat. Add the grated orange zest and the juice and season well.

Melt 2 tablespoons of butter in a small pan and toss the almonds until they are coloured. Remove and chop them, then stir back into the butter. Spoon the spinach mixture into the tomato halves and top with chopped almonds. Bake for 20 minutes. A red Valdepeñas *reserva*, made from Cenibel, which is the best of the Rioja grapes, will stand up well to the spinach.

PATATAS PICANTES

SPICY FRIED POTATOES

Potatoes fried in paprika are popular all over Spain and are one of the best-known dishes outside the country. This way of making them incorporates a little trick from the Canary Islands, where the potatoes are cooked in sea-water – theoretically until it evaporates – which leaves them crusted with salt and tasting delicious. The potatoes are then finished simply: just fried in oil and paprika. They are excellent with pork chops.

SERVES 4

500 – 700 g (1 – 1½ lb) new potatoes, (about 50 g [2 oz] each), scrubbed but not peeled
2 tablespoons coarse salt
4 tablespoons olive oil
4 fat garlic cloves
½ dried chilli, seeded and chopped, or a pinch of mild chilli powder
1 – 2 teaspoons paprika

Choose a wide saucepan and put in as many potatoes as will fit tightly in a single layer. Cover with cold water, add the salt and bring to the boil. Cover and cook for 20 – 25 minutes until done but not breaking up. Drain and peel or not as you wish, then cut into slices.

Heat the oil in a frying pan. Bruise the whole garlic cloves by pressing on them with the flat of a knife and add to the pan with the chopped, dried chilli, if using. When the garlic browns, discard the garlic and chilli.

Add the potato slices over medium-high heat. When they start to colour round the edges, sprinkle with the paprika, and chilli powder if using, and turn in the pan for a couple of minutes more. Because there is no chopped garlic in this dish, which would burn, the potatoes can wait in the pan over very low heat for 10 – 15 minutes.

GARBANZOS Y CHORIZOS

CHICKPEA AND SAUSAGE STEW

A dish from the chilly, wet region of Galicia, guaranteed to keep out the cold: my household eats it when we have been too long without Spanish food. Tolosa, in the Basque country, is famous for a similar dish made with black beans, while in Burgos pinto beans are used. Use whatever spicy sausages you can find – *morcilla* is often included as half the amount. With the modern short cuts of tomato juice and canned pimientos, the spicy base is very quick to make.

A good idea for supper with green salad and red wine, this is one of the few pulse dishes that reheats successfully. A little can be used in a *tortilla* and it's also good cold.

SERVES 4 – 6

500 g (1 lb) chickpeas, soaked for 1 hour in boiling water, or overnight in cold water

500 g (1 lb) cooking chorizos or other fresh spicy sausages, mild and hot together, in chunks

about 850 ml (1½ pt) unsalted stock, or one-third tomato juice, two-thirds water

1 large onion, chopped

2 garlic cloves, finely chopped

2 tablespoons olive oil

100 g (4 oz) canned pimiento or 2 tablespoons tomato paste (but not if using juice), plus 1 teaspoon paprika

salt and freshly ground black pepper

Drain the chickpeas, then simmer them in 1½ times their own volume of stock for ¾ to 1½ hours (depending on the brand, see page 11) until tender.

Fry the onion in the oil very slowly until soft, adding the sausage chunks after 10 minutes. Fry them for 20 minutes, turning them over occasionally. As they give off fat, add the garlic. When they are cooked, add them and their juices to the chickpeas.

Drain the pimientos, cut into strips and stir in (or add the tomato paste and paprika). Simmer for 10 minutes, season and serve.

GARBANZOS Y CHORIZOS *left,* MENESTRA A LA BILBAINA *right (p 67).*

ALCACHOFAS CON DOS SALSAS

ARTICHOKES WITH TWO SAUCES

The Spaniards admire the beautiful shape of artichokes and don't cut the leaves unnecessarily. It's more convenient for the eater, however, if the hairy choke is removed before they come to table. The cup this makes is then filled with mayonnaise, and there is vinaigrette for dipping the outside leaves. The same two sauces are often served with the white asparagus from Rioja, which is canned and sent all over the country.

SERVES 4

4 large globe artichokes
1 garlic clove, finely chopped
1 tablespoon finely chopped parsley
150 ml (¼ pt) mayonnaise (see page 78)
125 ml (4 fl oz) olive oil
3 tablespoons wine vinegar
salt and freshly ground black pepper

Snap off the stalks; with large tough artichokes this will bring away most of the stringy fibres underneath. Trim the bottom almost flat, removing little leaves. This will tell you how tender the artichokes are, and give you a better idea of cooking time. Cook tender heads for 20 minutes, and large tough ones for 40 minutes in plenty of salted boiling water. They will stay green if cooked without a lid. Drain them upside down for 10 minutes to cool a little.

To prepare them for the table, start by pulling out the centre leaves. When a soft, lighter cone becomes visible under the first leaves to go, hold the artichoke firm and pull the whole cone out. Underneath is the inedible hairy choke – scoop it out with a spoon. For decoration, turn the cone of small leaves over and lodge it in the artichoke to keep the cup open.

Eat barely warm or cold. To serve, stir a little garlic and parsley into the mayonnaise and fill each cup. Make a vinaigrette with the oil, vinegar and seasoning and pour a little on each individual plate. Eat the outside leaves, dipping each base into vinaigrette. Eat the inside ones – and finally the base itself – with mayonnaise. Remember to put out a plate to use for the discarded leaves.

ENSALADA DE NARANJAS VALENCIANAS

VALENCIAN ORANGE AND ONION SALAD

A Spanish storecupboard salad, from winter ingredients, it seems to have gone out of fashion somewhat, now lettuces and tomatoes are on sale all the year round. It is nevertheless excellent for adding a splash of colour to any meal and wonderful before a lamb stew. If green salads are available, decorate it with lettuce or *frisee* round the outside.

SERVES 6

4 large oranges
1 purple onion, or ½ mild Spanish onion
lettuce (optional)
2 tablespoons red wine vinegar

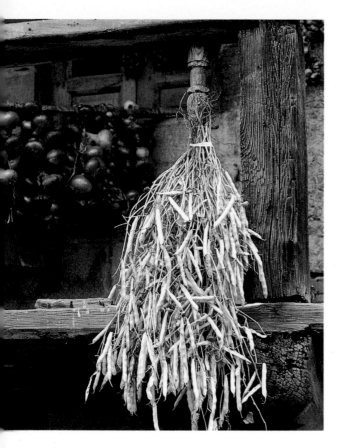

75 ml (3 fl oz) olive oil
salt and freshly ground black pepper
pinch of sugar
a few black olives

Purple onion rings look pretty but must be soaked in cold water for a couple of hours first, to tame their flavour. Slice the onion as thin as possible and push it out into rings, then leave to soak. Drain well on kitchen paper before use. Spanish onions are milder and need no soaking.

Peel the oranges, removing the membrane from the outside of the segments with the pith. Slice into rings and remove the pips. Arrange the orange and onion slices in a salad bowl. If using a deep bowl, line it with lettuce first, so a frill appears round the edge. If the bowl is wide and shallow, roll the lettuce leaves in wads, slice across and arrange the ribbons round the edge. Use the next 5 ingredients to make a vinaigrette and pour over the salad. Scatter with black olives and let it stand for 30 minutes before serving.

ESCALIVADA CON ANCHOAS

BAKED AUBERGINE AND RED PEPPER SALAD WITH ANCHOVIES

I suspect the reason why this exotic dish is unknown outside Spain is because its subtle colours photograph so badly. The aubergine turns a smoky grey-green and becomes unrecognizably soft, with prominent seeds which look fig-like. Spanish virgin oils, like Nunez de Prado or Sierra de Segura, are very fruity, and so make a good dressing.

Escalivar is the Catalan verb for 'cooking over the embers' and, on a barbecue, the vegetables pick up a smoky flavour. They make a popular garnish for grilled steak. Tomatoes and potatoes can be included too, and everything puréed (with a little cayenne if not using Spanish peppers). The resulting cream is chilled and served as a starter or as a sauce for fried sole.

SERVES 4

4 small aubergines, about 200 g (7 oz) each
4 red peppers
50 g (2 oz) canned anchovies, drained
4 tablespoons virgin olive oil

Heat the oven to 200° C (400° F, gas 6). Bake the peppers and aubergines on the wire shelf for 1 hour, turning them over at half time. When they are soft, transfer the peppers to a plastic bag.

Remove the stalks from the aubergines; the dark skin will come away easily. They will be soft and silky in texture, and only a quarter of their original weight. Split them into 4 to show off their exotic seeds. Remove the skin from the peppers, discarding stalks and seeds, and halve them lengthways.

Arrange an aubergine and a pepper on each plate (either side by side, or with the pepper on top like a sandwich) and criss-cross with anchovies. Dribble a little virgin olive oil over the salad.

DRYING BEANS *The number and variety of different beans in Spain – which are eaten fresh as well as dried – are truly astonishing. Each locality has its own, prized speciality.*

AMANIDA CATALANA

CATALAN ARRANGED SALAD

Amanida is the Catalan word for 'salad' and comes from *amanir*, 'to season', just as our own word comes from *sal*, 'to salt'. It is different every time, according to what is available.

We eat this salad for lunch most days in hot weather, choosing one group of ingredients only, with 3 or 4 items. The choice of ingredients is wide: for example, white canned asparagus can be substituted for the artichoke hearts, and goes well with mayonnaise and anchovies. Another happy combination is red mullet, cooked and dressed *en escabeche* (see page 118), with buttery avocados.

Arranged like the spokes of a wheel on a large plate, *amanida catalana* makes a dramatic buffet dish, or centrepiece for the first course of a dinner party.

SERVES 6

6 thin slices jamón serrano *or* prosciutto
6 bunches of tentacles cut from 500 g (1 lb) small squid, cleaned (see page 95) and rinsed
2 tablespoons olive oil
about 125 g (4½ oz) boiled prawns in the shell
2 cans (125 g [4½ oz]) sardines in oil, well drained
3 hard-boiled eggs, sliced
100 ml (3½ fl oz) thick mayonnaise (see page 78)
1 tablespoon large capers
400 g (14 oz) canned artichoke hearts, drained
3 pimientos from a 400 g (14 oz) can, well drained
12 king-sized green olives, about 75 g (3 oz)
18 small black olives, cured in oil, about 50 g (2 oz)
350 g (12 oz) ripe tomatoes, without skin or seeds, chopped into big dice
½ tablespoon very finely chopped parsley
flat parsley leaves
leaves from a frisee *or* lollo bianco *lettuce*
125 ml (4 fl oz) vinaigrette

Blot the squid tentacles well on kitchen paper. Heat the oil in a small frying pan and put in the tentacles, cut side down, so that they open like flowers. Fry them for a minute on each side, flipping them over so the other side turns pink. Drain on paper and reserve.

Cut the artichoke hearts into thirds lengthways and dress them, and the tomatoes, lightly with vinaigrette before you start the arrangement.

Arrange all the items on a large plate about 35 cm (14 in) across – I used a big glass shell-plate – or on individual salad plates. The various salads look best kept in groups, rather than dotted around. Spokes of a wheel look good on a big round plate and a fan shape on individual plates.

Cut the raw ham in half across the middle and roll up each piece so it has a frill of fat at the top. Arrange the ham rolls in a wedge and heap the tomato next to them. Scatter lightly with chopped parsley and pile the black olives next to the tomato.

Arrange the sardines all together, overlapping slightly in a wedge, with the tails towards the centre of the plates. Slice the pimiento in strips, and arrange next to them. The two red salads – pimiento and tomato – should always be separated.

Put the sliced eggs next to the sardines. Add the capers to the mayonnaise and pile half over the eggs, with the green king-sized olives towards the centre. Add the artichoke hearts as another wedge.

Arrange the prawns on the outside of the last section, with the squid flowers inside them. Finally, tuck a tiny bunch of *frisee* or lettuce between each section on the outside rim of the plate, and put some flat parsley leaves in the centre. The whole thing is so ornamental and delicious, I would add to the festive mood with Cava, the sparkling Catalan wine made by the champagne method. Codorníu and Raimat both have Cavas made from Chardonnay grapes.

PIRIÑACA

PEPPER SALAD WITH TUNA AND EGG

The dressing of this chopped salad has a much longer history in Spain than the vegetables it garnishes. Far older than mayonnaise, it is made with oil and the yolks of hard-boiled eggs.

Jaén, in the north of Andalusia, is famous for a very similar salad called *pipirrana*, which contains cucumber as well, but not necessarily tuna. Well chilled – and so a hair's breadth away from *gazpacho* – *pipirrana* accompanies slices of raw ham.

SERVES 6–8

3 small or 2 large eggs
200 g (7 oz) canned tuna in brine, well drained
3 small green peppers, stalk and seeds removed
3 fat ripe tomatoes, without skin, quartered
1 garlic clove, finely chopped
1 thin slice stale bread, without crusts
1½ tablespoons red wine vinegar
3 tablespoons olive oil
salt and freshly ground black pepper
flat parsley leaves, if available, or lettuce leaves

Hard boil the eggs for 12 minutes, drain and immediately cover with cold water to stop the yolks greying. Turn the tuna into a wide bowl and shred it with a fork. Quarter the pepper and scrupulously remove all the ribs inside. Cut into long thin shreds (double matchstick width) and then into neat dice. With a sharp knife, take out the insides of the tomatoes. Slice and then dice the quarters. Chop the hard egg whites the same size (reserve the yolks), mix everything together and chill.

Soak the bread in water, then squeeze out. Work the garlic to a paste with the salt and hard-boiled egg yolks in a small blender. Add the bread, vinegar and pepper and purée again. Work in the oil and purée to a smooth cream. Dress the salad 30 minutes before serving, tossing it gently, and pile on individual salad plates. A flurry of single flat parsley leaves makes a pretty garnish, as does a curly lettuce leaf.

ENSALADILLA

'LITTLE' OR 'RUSSIAN' SALAD

This little salad is peculiarly suited to Spain. It probably dates back to the Napoleonic wars, when so many Frenchmen took up residence in Spain, at a time when food 'in the Russian style' was all the rage in Paris. It is a regular in *tapas* bars.

For a cold lunch dish, serve with tuna-stuffed eggs – another Spanish invention. I also have a modern recipe from Algeciras, which adds a little curry paste to the mayonnaise and 250 g (8 oz) of peeled prawns to the salad ingredients.

SERVES 4

550 g (1¼ lb) potatoes, each about 50 g (2 oz)
1 large carrot, in big dice
3 tablespoons peas
1 green pepper, stalk, seeds and ribs removed
3 tablespoons mild Spanish onion, chopped to pea size
400 g (14 oz) canned artichoke hearts, quartered
1½ tablespoons capers
8 midget gherkins, chopped
8 black olives, 3 strips cut from around each stone
1 canned pimiento

MAYONNAISE
2 large egg yolks
2–3 tablespoons lemon juice
300 ml (½ pt) olive oil
1–2 tablespoons white wine or warm water
pinch of salt

Choose egg-sized potatoes and boil them in their skins (which tastes better) in salted water for 20–25 minutes. If they are larger than this, or peeled, the outside crumbles or the flesh gets too wet to make a good salad. Cool then skin the potatoes; slice them then chop to the size of bread cubes. Cook the carrots and peas. Cut the pepper into strips and dice it. Mix everything together, with the onion, artichoke hearts, capers and gherkins, seasoning well.

Make the mayonnaise. Put the egg yolks into a bowl with 2 teaspoons of lemon juice and the salt and whisk well. A hand-held electric whisk is easiest to use and will warm up yolks taken directly from the re-

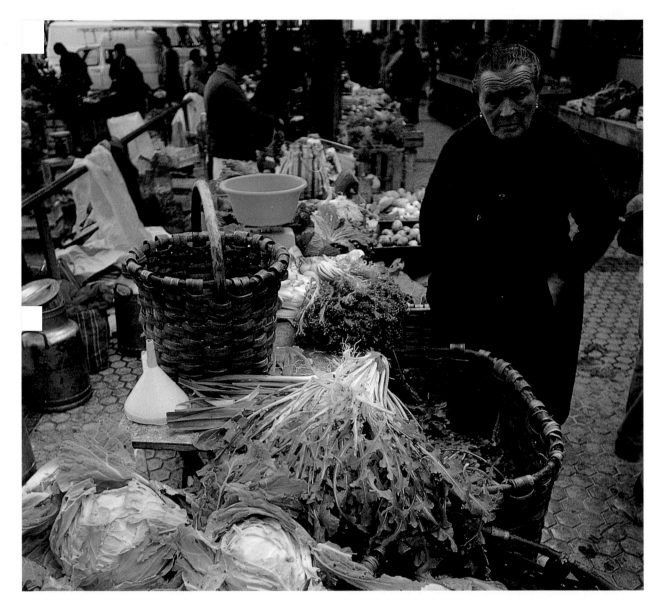

frigerator. Gentle warmth is the key to making an emulsion and so to easy mayonnaise. Spanish kitchens are always warm, but in an air-conditioned one, stand the measuring jug of olive oil in a pan of hot water.

Add about 2 teaspoons of oil at first, making sure it is blended before proceeding. Add a little oil at a time, beating in each batch. Finally taste and add seasoning. The mayonnaise will be a thick yellow butter, which can then be diluted with warm water, or in this case wine, to make the familiar cream for coating.

Pour the mayonnaise over the vegetables and toss

MARKET IN SAN SEBASTIAN *Sun-coloured Mediterranean vegetables like tomatoes and peppers are by no means used exclusively in Spanish dishes – abundant, glossy-leaved greens are equally valued.*

gently. Turn into a 1.5 l (2½ pt) loaf tin (pressing gently into the corners) or a gratin dish, and chill until needed. Work round the sides of the tin with a palette knife before turning out. If you wish, more mayonnaise can be spread on the outside – make a 3-egg-yolk quantity for this. Decorate with criss-cross strips of pimiento enclosing black olives.

FISH AND SHELLFISH

With Spain's thousands of miles of coastline and inland mountain streams, it is no surprise that the Spaniards' love of fish and shellfish knows no bounds.

VIEIRAS DE SANTIAGO *left (p 91)*, MERLUZA CON SALSA VERDE *right (p 83)*.

WITH COASTS ON TWO OCEANS, one brisk and cold, the other lazy and warm, the variety of Spanish fish and shellfish is enormous. Spain also has fast mountain streams teaming with salmon and trout. Eating fish and shellfish is a national passion.

The barbecue may just be a stick in the ground piercing a row of sardines by a beach fire, for the cooking in Spain is simple, but always appropriate. Plain frying, with a little lemon juice squeezed over afterwards, shows off varieties of fish hardly known outside the country. Skill at deep frying seems to be universal – golden crispness on the outside is the result, without a trace of oil. These traditional methods have been developed to show off simple flavours: like salmon, soaked in lemon, salt and milk, then grilled over charcoal, or brown trout, cooked in white wine, or wrapped in or stuffed with raw ham.

There are also the great soup-stews, encrusted with shellfish. On the north coast *caldeirada de pescado* throws together a variety of clawed and shelled creatures, with great chunks of fish, and the Catalan coast has the splendours of *zarzuela* and a similar, tomato-less dish called *suquet* or *susquet*.

Even inland villages have markets with wet piles of shimmering silver fish like sardines, a bewildering choice from the sea. The charmingly-named *salmonetes*, or red mullet, grilled without cleaning, are piled next to small brown sole, looking like lost shoes. Shark flesh lies skinned on the fish counters, pink and defenceless like great meat bones, destined to end up in stews. Steaks of swordfish, *pez espáda*, with its black plastic-like skin, are good for grilling.

The favourite of so many Spaniards is *merluza*, hake, loved for its delicate flavour and flaky texture, though hake recipes can be cooked with cod or haddock. Another famous Mediterranean fish is the *mero*, a grouper, and a proverb says that the best things to eat are 'the lamb from the mountain and the *mero* from the sea'. I suspect the Spaniards taught the rest of Europe to eat monkfish and you can see great saddles in the Boqueria market in Barcelona, ready for roasting.

Traditionally the Basques have been the Atlantic fisherman, adding another fish – cod – to the Spanish repertoire, since it is unknown in the Mediterranean.

The Basque speciality is *bacalao*, salt cod, with the local peppers, and *bacalao* is still extremely popular throughout the country, especially during Holy Week. The coming of frozen fish has made no dent upon what was, at one time, just a convenience food.

The diversity of the shellfish is amazing. Spain has many sorts of prawns, each with their own names. These are cooked and eaten simply, like the *gambas de Palomos*, which are boiled for exactly three minutes, then placed on ice to arrest further cooking. *Langostino* is one of the bigger prawns, though its name is deceptively close to the French *langoustine*, which is called *cigala* in Spain. This latter is a clawed salt-water crayfish, and is unusual in being pink and white even when alive at the market. *Langosta*, the spiny rock-lobster, is valued for the sweet meat which is all in the tail, and is normally boiled and served plain with mayonnaise.

The star of the north coast is *centolla*, the spider crab. It is stronger and sweeter than the clawed crab, but there is less meat, so this is normally mixed with hake, then stuffed back into its shell.

Both coasts have mussels in plenty and there are sea dates, sea urchins in their hedgehog shells and a huge selection of tiny clams, each with local names. *Navajas* are razor shells, and come from the market bundled with string, an occasional white tongue lapping out of a brown end. And strangest of all are barnacles called *percebes*, which stand from the rock like miniature black bear's claws, complete with white fingernails.

The *concha fina*, 'finest shell', of the south coast is a big Venus shell. The best place to eat these in is one of the sherry bars of Malaga, where an old man sits all day at the task of opening them. Here the sherry barrels are stacked to the roof, each with its grape scrawled across the butt. You may choose from this one, then that, while the huge shells are opened before you, a glory of scarlet and orange roes.

Squid are extremely popular, the more so as freezing does not spoil them. Fried rings of *calamares* are ubiquitous, but on the northern, Cantabrian coast, squid fried in breadcrumbs are sold as *rabas*. Cuttlefish is normally stewed. The rich sweetness of its black ink is featured in the exotic *sepia en su tinto* in the north and in the east coast rice dish, *arroz negro*.

MERLUZA
CON SALSA VERDE

HAKE WITH GREEN SAUCE

The green wine-and-parsley sauce of this famous Santander casserole is one of the nicest complements to the delicate flavour of hake. It is often served in individual casseroles and the sauce, which may be of soup proportions, may well include lots of fishy extras. Clams are traditional, and any shellfish that traps a little seawater inside its shell. Another version includes the Basque speciality *kokotxas*, or hake cheeks, a tiny 'oyster' of sweet flesh from beyond the fish's eye.

Doña Plácida de Larrea of Bilbao wrote to a friend in 1723, describing the dish, and added that her husband liked a light, sweetish white wine with it. Marqués de Cáceres make a light white Rioja that is the best wine in the new fresh, fruity style of white Riojas, none of which taste of oak casks, as they are not aged in wood.

SERVES 4

4 pieces of hake fillet, about 150 g (6 oz) each
250 g (8 oz) clams or cockles, rinsed
250 g (8 oz) mussels, cleaned (see page 96)
200 g (7 oz) shelled peas, cooked if fresh
1 onion, finely chopped
2 garlic cloves, finely chopped
2 tablespoons olive oil
2 tablespoons butter
2 tablespoons flour
6 tablespoons parsley
175 ml (6 fl oz) dry white wine, preferably Rioja
350 ml (12 fl oz) fish stock
salt and freshly ground black pepper

Heat the butter and oil in a casserole into which all the fish will fit comfortably and fry the onion gently until soft, adding the garlic near the end. Season the fish steaks and flour lightly. Push the onion to the sides of the pan and add the fish, skin up. Cook them slowly, turning them over once, until light golden.

Add the fish stock and white wine and bring to simmering point. Add the shellfish and, when the shells open, the peas, and simmer for 5 minutes. Stir in the parsley and check the seasoning. Serve in soup plates.

ESQUEIXADA

CATALAN SALT COD AND
PEPPER SALAD

Aficionados will tell you that *bacalao*, salt cod, is one of the great acquired tastes – like caviar or truffles. And this salad from L'Empordà, the Costa Brava region, will be a revelation to anyone who has not eaten dried cod before, and thinks they don't quite like the sound of it. The fish is translucent and mild, pickled by the vinaigrette, rather than cooked. The name of the dish comes from the Catalan verb 'to shred'.

SERVES 4 – 6

250 g (8 oz) thick salt cod, soaked for 48 hours
(see page 10)
¼ small onion, sliced very finely
2 red peppers, stalks and seeds removed
2 fat ripe tomatoes, without skin
3 tablespoons virgin olive oil
1 tablespoon red wine vinegar
freshly ground black pepper
50 g (2 oz) black olives to decorate

Drain the cod and then blot well with kitchen paper. If the flesh is chunky, cut it into strips and press gently in paper to remove the last water. Discard the skin, bones and any discoloured flesh and remove all membrane.

Shred the cod finely with your fingers – the result looks more like white mushrooms than fish. Add some slivered onion – the equivalent of $1\frac{1}{2}$ tablespoons. Combine the oil and vinegar and pour over. Sprinkle with pepper, toss and leave to marinate for 2 – 3 hours in a cool place.

Slice the peppers not much bigger than matchsticks and pour boiling water over them, to soften them a little. After 10 minutes, drain and dry on kitchen paper. Quarter the tomatoes and remove the inside with a knife. Slice the flesh neatly. Stir the fish and all the salad ingredients together gently. Arrange on side plates and garnish with black olives.

FRITOS DE PESCADO A LA MALAGUEÑA

MIXED FRIED FISH, MALAGA STYLE

Andalusia is sometimes called *zona de los fritos*: Cadiz, Malaga and the province of Murcia are all known for their superb fried fish. The elegant city of Malaga, which has survived the influx of tourists better than some others on the coast, is known for this sophisticated dish, with its different colours and textures. For four people, fry only three types of fish, omitting one variety of white fish and the squid.

SERVES 6

500 g (1 lb) lemon sole, or 250 g (8 oz) sole fillets
250 g (8 oz) hake, cod or haddock
3 × 175 g (6 oz) red mullet
250 g (8 oz) fresh anchovies, small sardines or whitebait
250 g (8 oz) small squid, cleaned (see page 95)
flour for dusting
150 – 175 ml (5 – 6 fl oz) olive oil for frying
2 lemons, cut in wedges
sprigs of flat parsley to garnish
salt and freshly ground black pepper

Skin the sole by laying them skin down and running a sharp knife between the skin and the flesh. Cut the sole into broad strips and the hake into chunks. Keep each type of fish in a separate pile.

Run a knife the wrong way along the mullet to remove all the sequin-like scales, then cut off the head and tail and gut the fish. Open them up and remove the backbones, pulling carefully at any bones round the stomach vent. Halve lengthways along the back, then cut each fillet into three. Clean and split the anchovies or sardines (see page 24): whitebait can be used whole.

When ready to cook, season and flour all the fish. Heat plenty of oil, preferably in several frying pans, and fry the fish, starting with the thickest and keeping the types separate. Turn them carefully until nicely cooked on each side and remove to drain on kitchen

FRITOS DE PESCADO A LA MALAGUEÑA

paper. A big *paella* pan or round serving dish is best for serving. Put in all the fish, each in a group, dividing each section from the next with lemon wedges, one turned up, the rest turned down. Put several parsley sprigs in the middle and serve immediately.

A good choice of white wine would be the long-established Marqués de Riscal, from Rueda. In a wire-covered bottle, originally intended to prevent tampering with the contents, it is made from one of the few Spanish grapes of character, Verdejo.

CARABINEROS CON WHISKY

LARGE PRAWNS WITH WHISKY

Their brilliant colour earns these scarlet 'guardsmen' their military name. This and their sheer size – up to 23 cm (9 in) long – command respect, but in fact their flavour is slightly less good than that of other large prawns. Brandy, rum and, in modern times, imported whisky, are therefore used to improve this. Substituting another variety of large prawn will make the dish even better.

SERVES 4

1 kg (2 lb) large raw prawns, shelled
3 – 4 tablespoons olive oil
1 onion, finely chopped
250 g (8 oz) ripe tomatoes, without skin or seeds, or 200 g (7 oz) canned tomatoes, with juice
¾ teaspoon salt
4 tablespoons Scotch whisky

Heat 2 tablespoons of oil in a frying pan and add the onion, cooking it slowly until softened. Add the chopped tomato and cook until it is reduced to a sauce. Push the sauce to the edges of the pan, add 1 – 2 tablespoons more oil and put in the peeled prawns. Cook for about 4 minutes, depending on size, stirring occasionally, and sprinkle with salt.

Warm the whisky in a ladle, set light to it and pour it over the prawns. Stir the prawns into the sauce and serve them at once.

PIXIN A LA ASTURIANA

MONKFISH IN APPLE AND CIDER SAUCE

Cider is firmly entrenched on the north coast of Spain: indeed, the Basques claim to have invented it. *Pixin* is the local Asturian name for monkfish, called *rape* elsewhere in Spain. It's one of the fish most solidly incorporated into Spanish cuisine, and its boneless flesh and shellfish-like taste have become fashionable elsewhere. The way the fried potatoes are soaked in the sauce, rather than eaten crisp, is typically Spanish.

The dish is excellent family fare cooked with any white fish like haddock.

SERVES 4

650 g (1¼ lb) monkfish on the bone
250 g (8 oz) small clams, rinsed
2 dessert apples (optionally 4)
1 onion, chopped
2 garlic cloves, finely chopped
1 ripe tomato, without skin or seeds, diced
1 teaspoon tomato paste
500 g (1 lb) potatoes, diced to the size of bread cubes
1 tablespoon lemon juice
about 2 tablespoons flour
100 ml (3½ fl oz) olive oil
250 ml (8 fl oz) dry cider
pinch of cayenne pepper
salt and freshly ground black pepper

Fry the onion in 2 tablespoons of oil in a saucepan. As it softens, add the garlic. Add the tomato flesh, cayenne and cored, chopped apples. Stir in the cider and cook for 15 minutes. Check the seasonings, adding the tomato paste if the tomato was not large or ripe enough, and purée everything in a blender. Return to the pan. Heat the oven to 180° C (350° F, gas 4).

Heat 4 tablespoons of oil over medium-high heat in a frying pan and fry the potatoes, tossing them regularly. Reserve in the oven in an earthenware casserole or serving dish.

Remove the grey skin from the monkfish and also the less noticeable skin inside the belly cavity. Take the fish off the bone and portion it. Sprinkle the fish with lemon juice and season and flour it lightly. Add 2 more tablespoons of oil to the pan and fry the fish, turning, until golden. Transfer to the dish containing the potatoes. Reserve a quarter of the potatoes and fit the rest between the fish portions in the dish.

Reheat the sauce, adding the clams (which will open), and pour over the fish. Garnish with the reserved potatoes. Give the dish 10 minutes in the oven for the flavours to blend. Fried apple rings also make a good garnish. Spanish cider is rarely exported, so drink your own to accompany it.

TILED KITCHEN *Since the 13th century ceramics, particularly* azulejos, *glazed tiles, have been used in decoration.*

MARMITAKO

MACKEREL AND RED PEPPER STEW

A shipboard stew, eaten by Basque fishermen, *marmitako* is often made with tuna, but the dish is also a good way of eating the cheaper mackerel. Its name comes from the pot used for cooking it, better known to us by the French name of *marmite*.

Dry wine is needed in the recipe to balance the rich, sweet, piquant peppers and oily fish. Dry cider could also be used (and drunk with it, though Spanish cider is

rarely exported). If, however, you don't want to open a bottle, use instead the juice of 3 lemons or, more unconventionally, 2 limes. It's my belief the tomatoes are a recent addition, and that this is in fact the famous fish sauce that appears in Basque recipes *a la vizcaina*, most notably for *bacalao* or salt cod. Older recipes for *marmitako* talk of soaking the peppers in water for 24 hours and they were originally the only vegetable in the sauce. I might add that on boats nowadays, the *pimientos* come from a can.

SERVES 4 – 5

2 – 3 small mackerel (about 1 kg [2 lb] before
cleaning), filleted (or 550 g [1¼ lb] tuna)
3 large red peppers
1 onion, chopped
2 garlic cloves, finely chopped
400 g (14 oz) canned tomatoes, with juice
500 g (1 lb) potatoes, in small cubes
4 tablespoons olive oil
150 ml (5 fl oz) dry white wine
2 teaspoons paprika
1 dried chilli, seeded and chopped
salt and freshly ground black pepper
2 tablespoons chopped parsley

Quarter and seed the peppers, then pour about 1.75 l (3 pt) of boiling water over them and leave to soak and soften for 2 – 3 hours. Heat the oil in a large shallow casserole, big enough to take the fish. Fry the chopped onion gently, adding the garlic when it is nearly soft.

Cut each mackerel fillet into 3 or 4 pieces and season them well. Push the onion to the sides of the casserole, put in the fish and fry it on both sides.

Add the wine to the casserole with the pieces of dried chilli. Add the pulped tomatoes – on board ship this is done by squeezing each one in the hand and letting it run out through the fingers into the sauce. On dry land you can pulse them briefly in a food processor. Distribute the potato cubes over the top and sprinkle them with paprika and more salt and pepper.

Drain the red peppers, saving the liquid, then shred them (or process them briefly) and add to the pan with enough of the soaking liquid to cover the potatoes well. Cook for about 20 minutes, or until the potatoes are well done and the liquid is somewhat reduced. Check the seasonings, stir in the chopped parsley and serve the stew in soup bowls.

TRUCHAS CON SALSA ROMESCO

MOUNTAIN TROUT WITH PIQUANT ALMOND SAUCE

Thickened with hazelnuts and almonds combined with bread, this is one of the oldest ways of making sauce in Europe – a mountain sauce, in a country where hills face the coast at almost every turn. It's my belief that it was previously seasoned with black pepper, of which the Catalonians are extraordinarily fond. The red *romesco* pepper which now gives its name to the sauce was then introduced – along with the tomato – in the 16th century, resulting in a more successful version of the same peppery taste.

Called a *ñora* pepper in other parts of Spain, the *romesco* is spicy without really being hot. For those with access to Mexican stores, Colman Andrews, in *Catalan Cuisine*, suggests substituting ½ canned *jalapeño* chilli, plus 3 dried *ancho* peppers, although I could not find the latter. The *jalapeño*, however, was very good – I also recommend a little *jalapeño* ketchup.

Romesco makes an interesting accompaniment for roast chicken or a cold Christmas Eve salmon, but is most frequently served with fried fish. The sauce may then include the fried fish livers – often an unwanted gift from whole fish.

SERVES 4

4 trout, each 250–350 g (8–12 oz), cleaned
2 tablespoons melted butter
2 tablespoons olive oil
salt and freshly ground black pepper

SALSA ROMESCO

25 g (1 oz) almonds, blanched
25 g (1 oz) hazelnuts, blanched
250 g (8 oz) ripe tomatoes, without skin or seeds, or
200 g (7 oz) canned tomatoes, with juice
2 garlic cloves, finely chopped
6 tablespoons olive oil
1 slice of 1-day-old bread
2 teaspoons red wine vinegar
4 tablespoons fino sherry
pinch of cayenne pepper or 1 cm (½ in) piece of canned
jalapeño chilli, seeded

Start the sauce by toasting the nuts in a low oven – about 150° C (300° F, gas 2) – for 20 minutes, until biscuit-coloured. Heat 4 tablespoons of oil in a frying pan, frying the garlic while it heats; remove and reserve the garlic, then fry the bread briskly on both sides and reserve it.

Add 2 more tablespoons of oil to the frying pan, then the chopped tomatoes and cayenne or *jalapeño* chilli, stirring until much reduced. Grind the nuts in a blender, then add the bread and garlic and pulverize them with the vinegar and sherry to make a *picada* – a piquant last-minute addition to the sauce. Stir this into the sauce. If you wish, the whole sauce can be blended once more to a pink 'mayonnaise', adding a few extra tablespoonfuls of oil.

Heat the grill to high. Wash the trout inside and out and salt and pepper them. Brush them with the butter and oil and grill for 5–7 minutes on each side, turning once. Serve on hot plates, with the sauce, accompanied by an aristocratic white Rioja in the old style, such as the *blanco reserva* from Marqués de Murrieta, which has some lemon acidity as well as an oakiness from the casks in which it is matured.

BACALAO EN SAMFAINA

SALT COD IN MIXED VEGETABLE SAUCE

The Basques cook *bacalao* with onions and the local peppers, which are bright red, sweet and a good deal more spicy than bell peppers. The result is called *bacalao a la vizcaina*, Spain's most famous salt cod dish.

When the dish is made outside the Basque country, however, the sauce often includes a great deal of tomato – perhaps to compensate for the lack of those famous peppers. I have therefore chosen a popular salt cod recipe with tomato sauce as its base, though lots of other vegetables are included too.

Samfaina is one of Spain's best-known sauces. A vegetable dish in its own right when served by itself or with pork chops, it is often cooked with chicken.

In spite of the better roads that have been built in the Pyrenees, access to many hamlets and villages remains difficult and here life – and cooking methods – have changed little over the centuries.

SERVES 4

500 g (1 lb) thick salt cod, soaked overnight (see page 10)

SAMFAINA

100 g (4 oz) smoked bacon or gammon (optional)
250 g (8 oz) aubergine, without stalk or skin
1 large onion, chopped
2 garlic cloves, finely chopped
2 red peppers, seeded and cut in squares
750 g (1 lb 6 oz) ripe tomatoes, without skin or seeds, or 600 g (1¼ lb) canned tomatoes, with juice
1 large courgette, cubed with the skin on
1 bay leaf
175 ml (6 fl oz) dry white wine
about 125 ml (4 fl oz) olive oil
salt and freshly ground black pepper

Cube the aubergine, sprinkle with salt and leave to stand in a colander for 30 minutes. Remove the skin and all the bones from the salt cod, discarding any discoloured flesh. Cut the fish into 'fingers', following the natural shape, and blot well with kitchen paper.

Start the *samfaina*. Heat 2 tablespoons of oil in a casserole big enough to take all the ingredients. Fry the onion and bacon or gammon, if using, over medium heat until the onion colours, then add the garlic. Add the peppers, tomato, wine and bay leaf and simmer gently, stirring occasionally, until the tomato has disintegrated into a sauce.

Meanwhile put 4–5 tablespoons of oil in a frying pan and fry the fish pieces on both sides until well-coloured and golden, then remove from the pan and add to the tomato sauce.

Rinse the salt off the aubergines and pat dry with kitchen paper. Add more oil to the frying pan if needed and fry the aubergine and courgette cubes gently, turning them occasionally. When they are golden, add to the tomato sauce and fish and simmer, covered, for 15 minutes: a little water may be needed. Check the seasoning and serve.

RAPE CON MAHONESA
Y ENSALADA DE ARROZ

COLD MONKFISH IN MAYONNAISE
WITH RICE SALAD

The Duc de Richelieu brought mayonnaise back to France after capturing the port of Mahon in Menorca in 1756. Did his chef invent it there, with local ingredients, or did he discover a Spanish invention? The Spaniards naturally favour a spelling of the sauce which emphasizes their role and Elizabeth David lends support to a local origin, in *French Provincial Cookery*: 'It certainly seems likely that by the 1750s the sauce was already known in Spain and Provence.'

In April and May when blood oranges are in season I add orange juice, cream and cayenne pepper to make pink mayonnaise for shellfish. But I was amused to find that even Michelin-starred chefs use a dab of tomato ketchup for the rest of the year. This is a really wonderful sauce for boiled lobster, but is more often eaten with rounds of monkfish, which superficially resemble lobster, or a combination of fish such as hake and prawns.

SERVES 4

700 g (1½ lb) monkfish on the bone
175 ml (6 fl oz) dry white wine
salt and freshly ground black pepper

PINK MAYONNAISE

100 ml (3½ fl oz) thick mayonnaise (see page 78)
2 tablespoons orange juice
1 tablespoon tomato ketchup
1 tablespoon thick cream (optional)
dusting of paprika

RICE SALAD

200 g (7 oz) long-grain rice
1 green pepper, stalk and seeds removed
500 g (1 lb) ripe tomatoes, without skin or seeds
4 tablespoons olive oil
2 tablespoons wine vinegar
1 garlic clove, finely chopped
½ teaspoon Dijon mustard
pinch of caster sugar
¾ teaspoon salt
freshly ground black pepper

Sprinkle the rice into plenty of boiling salted water, stir once and simmer for 15 minutes. Drain in a sieve, running cold water through it to remove starch, then bounce 2 – 3 times to drain the rice again. Spread it out on kitchen paper to dry.

Cut down on either side of the monkfish bone and remove it. Peel away all skin, including the white belly skin, and lay the fish fillets head to tail in a small oval pan or casserole. Cover with white wine and bring gently to simmering point. Cook for 8 minutes then drain and cool.

Cut out the ribs from the pepper, then slice and cut into small dice. Quarter the tomatoes, cut out the insides then dice. Make a dressing from the remaining salad ingredients, then season the rice and stir in the peppers and dressing. Add the tomatoes only at the last moment, as they may ooze juice into the rice.

Trim any loose bits off the fish (chopping them into the rice) and then cut each fillet into 8 neat rounds. Mix the flavourings into the mayonnaise – the cream can be whipped if it is thin. Make a rice bed on a serving dish and arrange the monkfish on top, coating each piece with mayonnaise. Sprinkle the fish very lightly with paprika. This is an easy summer dish, so drink with it an easy summer white wine. Fresh, dry and a little lemony, Torres Viña Sol is not aged and is the best of the white wines made exclusively from Parellada, the Spanish grape, but in the new French style.

VIEIRAS DE SANTIAGO

ST JAMES' BAKED SCALLOPS

Scallops in Galicia are huge – often monster 8-year-olds, so a single one makes a portion. Every restaurant in the old town of Santiago seems to offer this dish on St James' Day: a pleasant variation on the white wine and mushroom *coquilles St-Jacques*.

SERVES 4

*400 g (14 oz) scallops off the shell or, preferably,
2–3 good-sized ones on the shell per person
1 onion, finely chopped
3 garlic cloves, finely chopped
200 g (7 oz) ripe tomatoes, without skin or seeds, or
175 g (6 oz) canned tomatoes, with juice
125 ml (4 fl oz) white wine or good fish stock
4 tablespoons aguardiente, Fundador or another
Spanish brandy
1 tablespoon butter
3 tablespoons oil
1 teaspoon paprika
pinch of cayenne pepper or ½ dried chilli, without
seeds, chopped
salt and freshly ground black pepper
2–3 tablespoons fine breadcrumbs
1 tablespoon finely chopped parsley*

WINDOW IN GRANADA *Stucco decoration adds a splash of colour.*

ZARZUELA (overleaf) *(p 94)*.

If buying scallops on the shell, also ask for the curved, deep upper shell. To clean the scallops, hold a knife flat against the shell and cut the flesh free, then remove the ring of gristle that often surrounds the white. Separate large corals, which take only seconds to cook, from the white. Shelled scallops may need cleaning by pulling away any dark gut at the root of the coral, but more often they are coral-less.

Heat the butter with a tablespoon of oil and quickly fry the white parts of the scallops in butter for 2 minutes on each side. The corals are then added and just flipped in the hot butter. Shelled or defrosted scallops tend to make a lot of liquid, so remove them when cooked and boil this off. Warm the *aguardiente* or brandy, flame it and pour over the scallops. Spoon them into the upper shells or small heatproof dishes.

Add 2 tablespoons of oil and fry the onion gently until soft, adding the garlic towards the end. Add the chopped tomato, paprika and cayenne or chilli and cook to reduce. Moisten with the wine or fish stock, season and spoon over the scallops. Mix the breadcrumbs and parsley together and sprinkle thinly over the top. Heat through for 2–3 minutes under a low grill and serve immediately.

Tomato and brandy make this a rich dish and if it is a starter choose a dry *fino* or *amontillado* sherry to accompany it. If the scallops are a main course, partner them with an oaky white Rioja *reserva*, like the classic Marqués de Murrieta.

ZARZUELA

A MEDLEY OF FISH

A *zarzuela* is a theatrical performance, a combination of light opera and witty, satirical comedy. It took its name from the Zarzuela, the King's informal home in Madrid. This Catalan dish evokes the operetta, for it is another wonderful mixture – this time of tastes and colours, shapes and textures – and the flaming alcohol poured over it makes its own *coup de théâtre*.

To put on the performance, the various acts need a little planning. It's a 3-pan job (4 if your casserole is not table-worthy), but it is not difficult to do. Look for an anis-scented alcohol: colourless *aguardiente* is ideal. I also like *pacharán*, which is like an anis-scented brandy, made from sloes and normally drunk 'on the rocks'. Zoco is the best-known brand and flames beautifully. It is rather like a brown, sweeter version of Pernod. However, some exported *pacharáns* are lower in alcohol and this has to be boiled off.

The dish will serve six people as a starter, four as a main course.

SERVES 4

4 langoustines (Dublin Bay prawns with their heads) or king prawns
250 g (8 oz) mussels, cleaned (see page 96)
250 g (8 oz) clams (or extra mussels), rinsed
350 g (12 oz) white fish, in 4 portions
4 small squid, cleaned (see page 95)
100 g (4 oz) medium-sized prawns in the shell
100 g (4 oz) small shrimps
1 onion, chopped
1 garlic clove, finely chopped
3 tablespoons chopped parsley
350 g (12 oz) ripe tomatoes, without skin or seeds, or 300 g (10 oz) canned tomatoes, with juice
5 tablespoons olive oil
2 bay leaves, crumbled
1 g packet of saffron
125 ml (4 fl oz) fino sherry
125 ml (4 fl oz) Pernod, Spanish brandy or pacharán
600 ml (1 pt) good fish stock
salt and freshly ground black pepper

Heat the stock with the sherry and bay leaves in a saucepan and put in the mussels. Cover and cook for a couple of minutes until they open. Remove the mussels and add the clams. Remove the empty top shells from both shellfish and reserve the stock.

Start the sauce base. Heat 2 tablespoons of oil in a large casserole, big enough to take all the shellfish. Fry the onion gently until soft, adding the garlic, then the parsley towards the end. Add the chopped tomatoes and let them reduce to a sauce.

Heat 3 tablespoons of oil in a frying pan. Season the fish pieces and then fry over medium heat, turning once, until light golden. Add the squid rings and tentacles and fry briefly. Heat the Pernod, brandy or *pacharán* in a ladle and, standing well back, set it alight and spoon over the fish until the flames die down. Or boil the *pacharán* then pour over.

Dissolve the saffron in a little of the stock, then stir the saffron and stock into the casserole. Bring to simmering point then add the *langoustines* and any raw prawns. Cook them for 5 minutes, then add cooked prawns and shrimps. Fit the fish pieces and juices into the casserole, with the squid, then add the clams and mussels. Simmer gently for a couple of minutes, then serve in soup plates.

Put out plenty of paper napkins, nutcrackers and spare plates for the shells. To eat *langoustines*, first pull off the head and suck the inside. There may be some meat inside big claws, so these are worth cracking, but there is nothing in the legs. Hold the body with finger and thumb on either side and press together to snap the stomach shell. Then peel the legs up over the back, like a prawn, to remove the shell. Pinch the tail hard to release the vacuum then pull the body out of the remaining shell.

Torres Gran Viña Sol 'Green Label' is a rich white wine with enough character to stand up well to the assortment of flavours. It contains some Sauvignon grapes and has a hint of oak casks about it.

94

SEPIA GUISADA CON ALBÓNDIGAS Y GUISANTES

CUTTLEFISH WITH MEATBALLS AND PEAS

The Catalans invented 'surf and turf' to eke out one expensive ingredient with another cheap one – originally the festive chicken with the free lobster, a combination which is now enjoyed all over the world. The same idea is behind this dish from L'Empordà, between Barcelona and the French frontier. It could be nicknamed 'poor man's veal' for it's rather like eating veal served two different ways.

Buy a large cuttlefish if you can, for its flesh is thicker and sweeter than squid, or buy one of the big squid fished in northern waters. If using small squid, keep the tentacles for a pretty salad and use only the bodies in this recipe.

SERVES 4

700 g (1½ lb) big cuttlefish or squid
400 g (14 oz) peas, fresh or frozen
1 onion, chopped
6 garlic cloves, finely chopped
3 tablespoons finely chopped parsley
100 g (4 oz) ripe tomatoes, without skin or seeds
400 ml (14 fl oz) meat or chicken stock
125 ml (4 fl oz) dry white wine
1 slice of stale bread
125 ml (4 fl oz) olive oil
1 tablespoon flour
salt and freshly ground black pepper

MEATBALLS

200 g (7 oz) lean pork, minced
200 g (7 oz) beef mince
2 slices of stale bread
50 ml (2 fl oz) dry white wine
2 tablespoons finely chopped onion
1 tablespoon finely chopped parsley
freshly grated nutmeg
½ teaspoon coarse salt
freshly ground black pepper
1 large egg, beaten, for coating
flour for coating

To clean squid, grip the tentacles and use them to pull out the insides. Cut across above the eyes and discard everything below. Large squid (and cuttlefish) have a mouthpiece in the centre of the tentacles which can be popped backwards like a button. Flex the body gently and the spinal structure, like transparent plastic, will pop out. Cuttlefish are very similar, except the body looks like a plump money purse with a frill round it, instead of a rocket with fins. Slit the body up both sides and remove the cuttle bone. Wash squid and cuttlefish well inside under running water. Rub off the skin with salt-coated hands and wash again. Cut the body into squares the size of large postage stamps and the tentacles of large shellfish into short lengths.

Make the sauce in a deep casserole without too big a base. Heat 3 tablespoons of oil, fry the bread over high heat till golden and remove to a blender. Fry the onion gently until it starts to soften then add the garlic and parsley. Add to the blender and reduce everything to a purée – this is the *picada*.

Sprinkle the flour into the casserole (more oil may be needed) and cook over medium-high heat until it turns brown. This is important to give the sauce its dark meaty taste, but be careful that it does not burn. Add the chopped tomatoes and stock and simmer to reduce. Traditionally the *picada* is added to thicken the sauce and then the whole thing is sieved. The easier way, however, is to add the contents of the casserole to the blender and purée everything once more. Return the sauce to the casserole, add the prepared shellfish and season with salt and pepper. Simmer for 15 minutes, or for 30 minutes if using frozen peas.

Make the meatballs. Sprinkle the bread with wine, then squeeze it out lightly and combine all the ingredients, seasoning well. Make large marble-sized balls and roll them in beaten egg. Transfer them to a plate covered with plenty of flour and shake it to and fro until the balls are coated. Heat 3 tablespoons of oil in a frying pan and fry the balls over high heat, shaking frequently so they colour and crisp on all sides.

Add the wine and peas to the casserole and cook till the peas are tender (20 minutes for fresh peas, 5 for frozen). Slip the meatballs into the sauce, bring back to simmering point and give them a minute or so in the sauce. Long-grain rice makes a good partner.

MEJILLONES
A LA MARINERA

SAILORS' SPICY MUSSELS

The Galician seaboard not only provides Spain with over a quarter of its national fish catch, but also gives the region the damp, misty weather that makes warming dishes particularly appreciated in its cooking.

Comforting and spicy on a cold day, I first ate these mussels in blustery weather at Muros, a small port on the way to the Atlantic outpost of Cape Finisterre – once considered the outpost of the world.

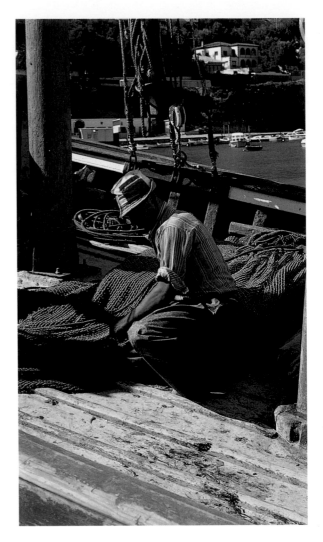

MENDING NETS IN LEVANT PORT *As well as the cooler Atlantic ports, Spain has all the variety of the warm Mediterranean to choose from, making it nothing short of a fish lover's heaven.*

SERVES 4

1.4 kg (3 lb) large mussels
1 small onion, chopped
1 garlic clove, finely chopped
½ bay leaf, crumbled
1 tablespoon flour
1 teaspoon tomato paste
½ teaspoon paprika
tiny pinch of cayenne pepper or mild chilli powder
1½ tablespoons olive oil
125 ml (4 fl oz) dry white wine
salt
1 teaspoon lemon juice

Cover the mussels in cold water and scrub the shells, discarding any that are smashed or do not shut when touched. Pull off all 'beards'. Do not clean them too far ahead, as this removes their life support system and they die.

Heat the wine in a saucepan with a lid and add the mussels in 3–4 batches. Cook briefly, covered, and remove them when they open, discarding any that remain shut. Reserve the liquid. Remove the top shell and arrange the biggest mussels in an ovenproof dish. Use a loose shell to cut the smaller bodies free and put 2 bodies in each shell.

For the sauce, fry the onion in the oil in a small pan, adding the garlic and then the flour when the onion softens. Cook briefly. Meanwhile boil the mussel liquid down to about 175 ml (6 fl oz), then add it to the pan with the bay leaf. Bring to simmering point, taste and add the tomato paste, paprika, cayenne and a little salt and lemon juice, as needed. Strain the sauce through a sieve then pour it over the mussels and heat them briefly (5 minutes under a low grill or in a medium oven). As the mussels are distinctly spicy, Spain's best-known lager, San Miguel, which has plenty of flavour of its own, would make a good thirst-quencher.

PULPO A LA FERIA

FESTIVE SPICED OCTOPUS SALAD

Octopus is very popular in the north of Spain and on St James' Day octopuses stand on all the bars in Santiago, purple-red but unthreatening. They look like great pincushions, or pink wigs standing propped ready-for-use on hat stands, a mass of pink rings curling away on all sides. Beside each one there is invariably a great stack of wooden plates, on which they are traditionally served.

It's difficult to decide whether the flesh tastes more like rabbit, chicken or tuna: it is white and firm, and Spanish cooks add a few bottle corks to the water when cooking, to make it more tender. This appears to work and is easier than tenderizing it by throwing or thumping it.

SERVES 4 – 6

750 g–1 kg (1¾–2 lb) octopus
1 large onion
1 garlic clove, finely chopped
75 ml (3 fl oz) olive oil
1 teaspoon paprika
2 pinches of cayenne pepper or a little mild chilli powder
coarse salt
freshly ground pepper
flat parsley leaves to garnish

Octopus is always displayed upside-down and inside out. To clean it, stretch out the tentacles and the bag which is the head. Make a cut round the head above the eyes and pull gently to remove the organs inside the head. Discard these, with the inksac. Turn the body inside out and wash thoroughly. Work round the beak in the mouth with a little knife and cut this out too.

Dip your hands in coarse salt and rub down the tentacles to remove all the skin. This is tougher than the membrane on squid, and comes away with a little flesh on the inside. Each sucker contains a little ring

RETURNING FROM MARKET *Supreme freshness in fish is highly prized and a fish that a short time ago was swimming in the sea may in a matter of hours have been caught, bought from the market and simply prepared, in just the way to bring out its natural flavours.*

and big ones will need popping out with finger and thumb, like a pop-it button.

In Spain octopus is beaten against an outside wall to tenderize it, but it is simpler to thump it with a bottle, turning it several times. Wash it again and split into individual tentacles. Drop the octopus into boiling water containing the onion and a bottle cork, and simmer until cooked, (about 45 minutes): test to see if it is slightly more tender. Turn off the heat and let it sit in the water for another 15 minutes.

I've eaten it spooned directly from the pot and dressed, but it is normally served as a salad at room temperature. Chop the tentacles into short lengths, combine all the dressing ingredients in a serving bowl and taste: it should be quite piquant. Toss the pieces. Arrange a few curly tentacle tips on top, sprinkle with parsley leaves and serve warm or cold.

MEAT,
POULTRY AND
GAME

---

*Succulent roast meats are often prepared for
festive occasions and imaginative poultry and
game dishes are delicious everyday fare.*

CORDERO ASADO CON ALIOLI DE MEMBRILLO *(p 101)*.

No cuisine in Europe is so distinctive as Spanish meat cookery. Strong on game, poor on beef, it has a long and different tradition. The Moors left behind a liking for spices, above all cinnamon, saffron and, nowadays, paprika, which appear in many sauces along with the beloved almond. Then there is the Arab taste for sweet-and-sour, which was given new impetus with the coming of the sweet red pepper. There is also a sophisticated appreciation of fat, which is exactly balanced by acidity in a dish such as duck *a la sevillana*, where bitter orange juice and olives counteract the natural fat of the bird.

Festive cuisine, with its superb roasts and grills, is the most immediately appealing. Exquisite lamb, grazed in the mountains of central and western Spain, is the luxury meat. Milk-fed lambs and *chotos*, kids, so tiny that a leg is a portion, are Easter fare, and no-one who has easten a roast from a great bread oven, like those at Haro or Aranda de Duero, will ever forget it. Sucking pig, just three weeks old, is marketed at Christmas-time. It's a speciality in places like Segovia, where the restaurateur Cándido used to carve it with the edge of a plate to demonstrate its tenderness. Spit-roast chickens are on sale in public squares on any weekend in the south. Roast game birds, stuffed with their own giblets, may well be the Sunday dish of rural families.

In restaurants in towns you will see the middle classes eating enormous beef steaks, *solomillos* and *chuletones*, but these are not village fare. Rather diminutive lamb chops barbecued over vine prunings are the real luxury, and pork the more common choice. The *solomillo andaluz* is not beef but from a pig, and the adage for grilling is 'lamb bloody and pork burnt'.

La plancha is used even more than the grill: this is a griddle that lies over the charcoal in every traditional Spanish kitchen and is built-in on modern cookers. On this *chuletas de cerdo*, pork chops, are cooked, with a dusting of paprika.

Another old-fashioned cooking tool is the pot for boiling meat. 'No violets come up to the perfume which a coming *olla* casts before it,' said Richard Ford. Also called a *puchero* – and *escudella i carn d'olla* in Catalonia – every region has its version. A more fanciful name is *olla podrida*, literally 'rotten pot', because long cooking softens the meat to the texture of overripe fruit.

If there is a national dish, then this is it. Called a *cocido* in Madrid, meats of different origin are simmered through the day – yet there is nothing of a stew or a sauce about this dish, but clean, elemental flavours. It also produces a wonderful clear broth, *caldo*, which is served as soup. This *cocido* is Jewish in origin: a pot left to simmer for the whole of the Sabbath. It was adopted after the Jews were expelled from Spain in 1492. Pork and sausages were then added, and its almost pure meat content made it an aristocratic dish. In the 18th century, chickpeas and potatoes went in too and, as a consequence, it slipped down the social scale. The pot provided more than one course and half a week's meals, for the meat from one day was cooked again on the next, in *ropa vieja*, leftovers, or literally 'old clothes'.

Good stews are a rural tradition, often of game birds or rabbits, which are free. *Carne de buey*, mature ox meat, and *carne de vaca*, from cows, both stew well, while *rabo de toro al Jerez*, bull's tail braised in sherry, is the most famous dish to come from the bullfight. However *toro de lidia*, meat from fighting bulls, may not be sold in ordinary butchers. *Ternera*, often translated as veal, is neither aged, hung beef, nor pink veal, but comes from steers killed between one and two years old. As minced meat, it is used for the popular *albóndigas*, meatballs, and for stuffings.

'It is not at all uncommon to meet adults among the peasants who have never tasted meat, except bacon, the *chorizo* or a wild bird,' reported *A Vagabond in Spain*, 80-odd years ago. These three still play an important role in the village kitchen. The pig is killed by a *matador*, like the bull, and the *matanza*, the slaughter which traditionally happens in mid-November, supplies cheap cuts for salting and a range of different sausages to last the winter, as well as the prized, gourmet raw ham.

Other traditional cured meats are still in demand for classic dishes like the Galician *lacón con grelos*, cured pork knuckle with turnip tops. The pig is also a great provider of fat, which makes plain vegetables appear richer than they are.

As people have become more prosperous, dishes based on the innards of animals or fowls have not been discarded. *Callos*, stewed tripe, remains a popular *tapa*. In village restaurants things like jellied trotters with chickpeas or *chanfaina*, a stew of all the pig's innards, from Extremadura, are still in demand. Liver, *higado*, in particular is served simply or included in many dishes with the meat it comes from, while kidneys in sherry are world-famous.

CORDERO ASADO CON ALIOLI DE MEMBRILLO

ROAST LEG OF LAMB WITH QUINCE ALIOLI

Roast lamb is quintessentially Spanish, and a luxury there as it is here. The unusual fruit butter that accompanies this dish comes from the Pyrenees, and illustrates the Catalan capacity for combining unexpected ingredients with brilliant results. No wonder they have taken to *nouvelle cuisine* so well! The sauce can also be made with pears, and prune *alioli* is a wonderful fruit butter for roast turkey.

The leg should be small — and ideally butchered along the natural lines of the animal to take in the whole bone — otherwise shortcut. Do not use a frozen leg, defrosted.

SERVES 6

1 leg of baby lamb, 1.3 – 1.6 kg (3 – 3½ lb), at room temperature
2 garlic cloves, finely chopped
1 teaspoon paprika
¼ teaspoon rosemary
2 tablespoons oil
salt and freshly ground black pepper
175 ml (6 fl oz) red wine

QUINCE ALIOLI

400 g (14 oz) stewed quince, or quince paste (dulce de membrillo in Spanish shops, cotognata in Italian delicatessens)
4 garlic cloves, finely chopped
½ teaspoon salt
1 tablespoon lemon juice (if using paste)
75 – 100 ml (3 – 4 fl oz) olive oil

Heat the oven to 230° C (450° F, gas 8). Remove any obvious lumps of fat from the underside of the lamb, which should be at room temperature. Crush the garlic to a paste with ½ teaspoon of salt, adding the oil, paprika and rosemary, and rub the paste all over the lamb. Put the joint in a roasting tin into which it fits fairly tightly, putting the trimmed fat and loose shank into the corner.

Roast uncovered for 15 minutes without opening the oven door. Then baste the lamb with the fat in the

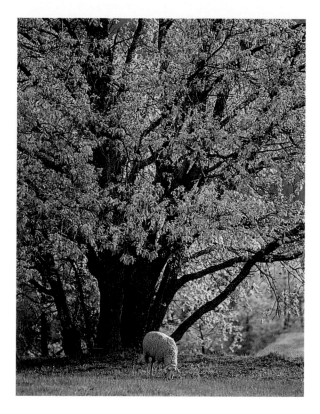

SHEEP GRAZING UNDER TREE *Grazing land is found chiefly in the mountainous areas of central and western Spain.*

tin, add the wine and baste again. Turn the oven down to 180° C (350° F, gas 4). Roast for 40–50 minutes for 1.3 kg (3 lb), 50–60 minutes for 1.8 kg (4 lb), basting once.

Meanwhile make the *alioli*. Crush the garlic and salt to a paste in a mortar. Be conscientious about this, to avoid small lumps. Put the drained stewed fruit into a blender with 2 tablespoons of its juice, or the quince paste with lemon juice, and reduce to a purée. Add the garlic paste and blend, then pour in the oil, a little at a time with the blender running. Fresh fruit makes a smooth pink 'mayonnaise'; quince paste is stronger and surprisingly good, despite the sugar.

Remove the lamb from the oven and leave to rest for 10 minutes. Drain the juices from the tin and skim all fat from the top. The carver should spoon a tablespoon or so of the meat juices over each portion. Serve the *alioli* in a sauce boat. A Cabernet Sauvignon goes well: those from Raimat in Lérida and Jean León in Penedès are red wine made locally, but from foreign grapes.

CORDERO
EN AJILLO PASTOR

SHEPHERDS' AROMATIC
LAMB STEW

The Romans introduced bread-thickened sauces and saffron to Spain, but the fondness for spiced food came from the Moors. This shepherds' stew, which comes from the hills above Jaén in Andalusia, has many aromatics and virtually no vegetables.

Lambs in Spain are killed when very young and in the hills the meat and bones would be chopped up together and would include some of the more perishable meats. You can replace the heart with extra lamb if you wish.

SERVES 6

1 kg (2 lb) cubed lamb, trimmed of fat and gristle
200 g (7 oz) lamb's liver, cubed
1 lamb's heart, split
2 slices of bread, torn in pieces
8 garlic cloves
15 black peppercorns
15 saffron strands or a 2 g packet of saffron powder
soaked in 2 tablespoons hot water
2 cloves
6 thyme sprigs or ½ teaspoon dried thyme
500 ml (16 fl oz) dry white Spanish wine,
or 50 ml (2 fl oz) dry sherry with 400 ml (14 fl oz)
dry white wine
1 tablespoon white wine vinegar
5 tablespoons olive oil
salt

Heat the oil in a flameproof casserole. Cut 6 of the garlic cloves in half or into thirds and fry with the cubed lamb in 2–3 batches over high heat, removing the lamb when browned. Meanwhile wash the heart inside and cut into meaty strips, discarding fat and any flaps. Add to the casserole with the liver and fry until coloured, then reserve with the cooked meat.

Fry the bread pieces in the oil remaining in the pan, with the 2 remaining garlic cloves, finely chopped. Transfer to a blender. Add the peppercorns, the saffron or saffron water, and vinegar and blend to a paste, adding a little wine if more liquid is needed.

Pour the remaining wine into the casserole and stir over low heat to deglaze the pan and pick up all the bits. Add this liquid to the blender and combine everything at low speed.

Return the meat to the casserole, season with salt, tuck in the cloves and thyme sprigs and pour the sauce over. Cook gently, covered, on top of the stove (or in the oven at 180° C [350° F, gas 4]) for about 45 minutes, until the lamb is tender and the sauce a little reduced. Serve with *patatas fritas*, chips.

In Spain the wine drunk with this would probably be the local red Jumilla, high in alcohol like many wines in the south, without much acidity. However, the dish is a good one and deserves a Penedès like Torres Gran Coronas, with an equal amount of body and fruit, but dry and better-shaped.

CARNE CON
CASTAÑAS Y PERAS

BEEF WITH CHESTNUTS AND PEARS

This lovely autumn beef stew has a nut sauce, typical of Catalonia. Here, however, the purée of almonds is augmented by fresh chestnuts, and with pears, which have an all-important touch of cinnamon.

SERVES 4

1.1 kg (2½ lb) braising beef, in slices
250 g (8 oz) chestnuts
4 pears, stewed with cinnamon and a little sugar
175 ml (6 fl oz) dry white wine
150 g (5 oz) ripe tomatoes, without skin or seeds
75 ml (3 fl oz) olive oil
6 toasted almonds (see page 88)
25 g (1 oz) stale bread, without crusts
1 garlic clove, finely chopped
1 tablespoon flour
salt and freshly ground black pepper

Make a slit in each chestnut and drop into a saucepan. Cover with water and bring to the boil. Simmer for 20 minutes. Meanwhile, heat the oil in a wide casserole.

Fry the bread and the garlic and reserve them.

Cut the beef across the grain into fingers. Salt and pepper them lightly and fry in batches, tossing so that the beef colours on all sides. Do not put too many in at once (if a juice forms, remove the batch and boil the liquid away). Return all the meat and add the wine and the same quantity of water. Cover and stew gently for 45 minutes, checking the liquid level occasionally.

Meanwhile prepare the sauce. Peel the chestnuts, removing the brown skin. Put 2 – 3 tablespoons of oil in a small pan and add the chopped tomato flesh. Let this reduce to a purée and sprinkle with flour. Grind the almonds in a herb mill or small blender with the fried bread and garlic. Stir this purée into the tomato mix. Check that the meat is cooked and its gravy well reduced. Stir in the tomato mixture and the crumbled chestnuts: the sauce should coat the meat nicely. Quarter the pears, removing the core. Add them to the casserole and heat through. An easy-to-drink local red wine is Raimat Abadia, made with half Cabernet Sauvignon grapes, though a Rioja *reserva* would go well.

TERNERA CON ALCACHOFAS A LA CORDOBESA

VEAL WITH ARTICHOKES FROM CORDOBA

The town of Montilla in Andalusia gave us the word *amontillado* for a certain style of strong, medium dry wine, though ironically we now associate it first with sherry. The wines from the Montilla-Moriles district are fortified in Spain, like sherry, and the popular Alvear *fino*, C.B., is used for both cooking and drinking. Exported Montillas are in the sherry styles but are unfortified and, as a consequence, cheaper than sherry. 'Pale dry' Montilla is excellent for cooking. It

blends beautifully with veal escalopes in this dish from the neighbouring town of Cordoba, though leftover roast pork is nearly as good.

SERVES 4

8 – 12 small veal escalopes, about 550 g (1¼ lb)
6 fresh globe artichokes or 400 g (14 oz) canned prepared bases
2 tablespoons olive oil
2 tablespoons pork fat or butter
1 onion, finely chopped
2 garlic cloves, finely chopped
125 ml (4 fl oz) pale dry or medium dry Montilla wine or good sherry
150 – 250 ml (4 – 8 fl oz) meat or chicken stock
salt and freshly ground black pepper

Prepare the artichokes. Snap off the stalks (if they are stringy, that means the artichokes are tough and need an extra 5 minutes' cooking). Trim the bottom flat, removing small leaves. Turn on the side and cut through the top leaves just above the choke, leaving a base about 4 cm (1½ in) deep. Then trim away the side leaves with a small knife until the white base shows through. Cook the bases in boiling salted water for 10 minutes. Drain upside down and cool for 10 minutes.

Flip off any soft leaf stumps with your thumb, revealing the choke. Use a spoon and your thumb to remove the hairy choke, leaving a smooth cup base. Depending upon the toughness of the vegetable, this needs about 5 minutes' more cooking, which in this recipe it gets once added to the veal. Otherwise braise it in a dish or in boiling water.

Heat the oil and fat or butter in a wide shallow casserole and fry the onion until softened (20 minutes on low heat) then add the garlic. Season the escalopes well then put in half of them, well spread out, and fry over high heat until coloured on both sides. Remove to a plate and fry the remaining veal. Then return all the veal to the pan and sprinkle with Montilla or sherry, boiling this away.

Add the stock – for canned artichoke bases use only half the stock. Bring to simmering point, add the quartered artichoke bases and cook for 5 minutes (or heat through if using canned bases). In Cordoba a dry Montilla would certainly be drunk with this dish, or Chiclana, the local sherry-like Cadiz white wine.

COCIDO MADRILEÑO

MADRID BOILED MEAT DINNER

A *cocido* is a magnificent mixture of meats, which blend and exchange flavours and make that broth which is the essence of Spanish soups. In the earlier part of this century, in most middle-class households *cocido* was a daily ritual, except for Sundays and feast days. It was made in working-class households, too, though it was a common practice to share the ham bone, which was boiled first in one pot then again in the next.

The recipe produces soup, a separate vegetable course, if you choose so to serve it, and a dish of meat and chickpeas, which is sometimes served as a separate course, with tomato sauce.

Exactly what goes into a *cocido* depends on what your butcher or supermarket offers. It's a waste, though, to use a roasting joint and tender chickens. This is a dish for tough meats, full of flavour and made tender only by long cooking. First, you need some salted meat: traditionally salt pork belly, but cured beef is a good choice; bacon in one piece; and gammon or ham on (or off) the bone. Secondly, a sausage, preferably a smoked one, and black pudding. Thirdly, a piece of fresh meat – a boiling chicken, fresh pork belly, or possibly a piece of mature shin of beef, replacing the cured beef. Finally half a meat bone and a trotter for a rich stock.

The green vegetables are cooked in a second pot with the sausages – which is fortunate, since most of us don't own one pot big enough for everything – so the main soup is flavoured with meat, instead of cheap, all-too-familiar cabbage.

500–750 g (1 – 1 lb 10 oz) cured brisket of beef (or silverside) in one piece

250 g (8 oz) salt pork belly, or streaky bacon in 1 piece, or fresh pork belly

600 g (1 lb 4 oz) knuckle gammon bone, with some meat attached

½ boiling chicken, or ¼ roaster as second choice

550–650 g (1¼ – 1½ lb) beef marrow bone, sawn across

1 pig's trotter, split

2 cooking chorizos or other smoked sausage, like kabanos

1 morcilla or 175 – 225 g (6 – 8 oz) black pudding, cut from a ring (skinned if this is in plastic)

250 g (8 oz) chickpeas

1 whole garlic bulb

2 bay leaves

8 black peppercorns, crushed

1 small onion, studded with 2 cloves

700 g (1½ lb) Savoy green cabbage (or spinach)

2 carrots, in big pieces

2 leeks, in short lengths

500 g (1 lb) small new potatoes: '8 the size of eggs'

2 tablespoons rice

salt

Pour boiling water over the chickpeas and leave to soak until needed. Put the salted meat – in this list, the brisket, salt pork belly or bacon, and gammon knuckle – into a saucepan and cover with cold water. Bring slowly to the boil and simmer for 5 minutes to remove excess salt, then drain.

The dish needs a large stockpot – at least 6 l (10 pt). Pack in all the meat, skin side down, with the beef bone. Fit the boiling chicken and trotter on top. Add the garlic bulb, bay leaves and peppercorns and cover with water. Bring to simmering point, skimming off any scum that rises. Drain and add the chickpeas, cover and simmer on the lowest possible heat for 1½ hours, checking occasionally that there is enough liquid.

If you have bought a roasting chicken, add it at this point, with the onion stuck with the cloves. No other vegetables go in this pot – otherwise it would be impossible to disentangle the chickpeas.

Start the vegetable pot. Quarter the cabbage, remove the core and put in all the vegetables with the sausages, *morcilla* and a little salt. Bring to the boil and simmer for 25 minutes, until the potatoes are cooked.

As soon as the vegetables are cooking, strain off enough broth from the meat pot – about 1.2 l (2 pt) – to serve as soup for the first course of the meal. Put this in a saucepan, bring back to the boil, sprinkle in the rice and cook for 15 minutes, then serve.

Drain the vegetables and sausages; slice the *morcilla* and *chorizos* and arrange on a plate with the potatoes. Serve this with the meat (or as a second course). Slice all the meats, remove the marrow from the bone and slice it into the chickpeas. Arrange the meats and chickpeas on a platter, moistening with a little broth.

Drink a red Rioja with Spain's national dish. The choice depends on your meat: good salt beef, strong *chorizos* and a powerful Savoy cabbage need the

MAN WITH A GUN IN LA MANCHA *Millions of birds pass over Spain on their migration to and from Africa and game such as partridges, pheasants, quail and rabbits is found in abundance.*

cigar-box flavours of Bodegas Bilbainas' Viña Pomal: their *reservas* are often more mature than other Riojas of their age, but not oaky. However if the balance of your dish is towards fresh pork belly, chicken and mild sausages, then choose the more elegantly composed Viña Arana from La Rioja Alta. Both wines have considerable acidity, but are smooth and firm, a characteristic of wine from the Rioja Alta district.

ALPARGATAS VALENCIANAS

LITTLE MEAT ESPADRILLES IN WINE SAUCE

These pork and ham patties from Valencia are unusual and rather fun. Made in advance, they are then served in a wine and cinnamon sauce.

An *alpargata* is a rope-sole – better known by its French name of *espadrille*. When they are fried, the patties do look very like rope-soles, because the coating of egg white fries in the characteristic ring pattern.

SERVES 4 – 6

350 g (12 oz) lean pork or veal, minced
125 g (4½ oz) raw ham, smoked gammon or back bacon, minced
75 g (3 oz) stale bread, without crusts
2 garlic cloves, finely chopped
3 tablespoons finely chopped parsley
3 large eggs
salt and freshly ground black pepper
75 – 125 ml (3 – 4 fl oz) olive oil for frying

CINNAMON AND WINE SAUCE

1 onion, chopped
1 garlic clove, finely chopped
2 tablespoons finely chopped parsley
1 tablespoon flour
200 ml (7 fl oz) good meat or chicken stock
200 ml (7 fl oz) oaky Spanish white wine, or a dry white wine mixed 3:1 with pale dry Montilla
1 bay leaf
⅛ teaspoon powdered cinnamon

If you are using a food processor, make the bread-crumbs first, then mince together the pork or veal and ham, gammon or bacon. Add the crumbs, garlic, parsley and 3 egg yolks, keeping the whites to use later for the coating. Mix everything together, seasoning well, to make a stiff pâté.

With your hands, shape the mixture into small sausages about 5 cm (2 in) long, then flatten into shoe shapes. Heat 3 – 4 tablespoons of oil and fry the patties, about 3 minutes on each side. Reserve them on a tray and chill for at least 1 hour.

For the sauce, soften the onion in 2 tablespoons of oil until golden, adding the garlic and parsley for the last few minutes. Tipping the pan, spoon out any visible oil then stir in the flour and cook for a minute. Stir in the stock, wine, bay leaf and cinnamon and simmer for 5 minutes.

About 15 minutes before serving, whisk the egg whites with a little salt until peaks form and coat the *alpargatas*. Fry for 2 – 3 minutes on each side, until coloured and heated through. Reheat the sauce in a large casserole, slip in the *alpargatas* in a single layer, and simmer gently for 10 minutes. Buttered courgette sticks make a good accompaniment.

FABADA ASTURIANA

ASTURIAN BEAN AND SAUSAGE POT

From the mountains of Asturias, one of Europe's wildest and least populated lands, *fabada* makes a warm winter lining for the ribs. A variety of local specialities go into this big bean stew. Oak-smoked fresh sausages, for example, and the popular local *lacón*. This is a smoked, cured pork knuckle (knee) from the front leg, plus some of the flesh above, sold as a 'hand of pork' if fresh. Salt-cured trotters and pig's ears or tails may also be included, with the hard *longaniza* sausage. Salt pork or cured beef make a less exotic substitute for them.

A variety of meats is one key to this famous dish. As in the French *cassoulet*, fat, salt and smoked meat should each be represented. The amount of meat should roughly equal that of the beans when cooked, and so should be three times their dried weight. The real secret of the dish, however, is to impregnate the vegetables with the meat flavours, by long, slow cooking. The meats are not there, like raisins in the pudding, as a reward for eating up the beans.

Faves are big fat white beans: butter beans are nearest to them. As they have a tendency to disintegrate with the long cooking, it's simpler to omit presoaking. Traditionally, though, the beans and salt meat are soaked together overnight (instead of blanching).

Pote asturiano is a very similar, but more soup-like, dish which I like because it includes some fresh vegetables. To make this, substitute potatoes for one-third of the beans and add 500 g (1 lb) cabbage, cut in wedges, near the end.

SERVES 6

800 g (1 lb 12 oz) dried butter beans, or other large white beans such as dried lima beans
700 g (1½ lb) salt pork belly (or salt brisket or silverside)
700 g (1½ lb) smoked gammon knuckle or hock, skin slashed
500 g (1 lb) cooking chorizos or other spicy smoked sausages, like kabanos
175 g (6 oz) smoked morcilla or other black pudding
1 bay leaf
6 black peppercorns, crushed
1 teaspoon paprika
2 g powdered saffron (or substitute another 1 teaspoon paprika)
4 garlic cloves
2 tablespoons oil (optional)

Use a stockpot or large casserole of a minimum size of 6 l (10 pt). In a bowl cover the beans with plenty of boiling water. Put all the salt meat – the pork belly and gammon or ham bone – into a pan and cover with cold water. Bring to the boil, then drain the meat and put it into the casserole.

Drain and add the beans, bay leaf, peppercorns, paprika and saffron. Add 2.3 l (4 pt) water – beans will absorb 3 times their own volume. Bring slowly to the boil, then simmer very gently on minimum heat for 2 hours – a big pot on a small burner is best, and better still with a heat diffuser. Check occasionally that the beans are still covered, but do not stir. They need very gentle cooking to prevent them breaking up.

Remove the gammon or ham bone and salt pork to a board, to cool a little. Strip off the skin and fat, and take about 2 tablespoons of chopped fat for frying (or use oil). Put this in a frying pan and sweat until it gives off enough fat for frying. Fry the garlic lightly, then spoon it into the beans. Add the sliced sausages and black pudding to the frying pan. Fry lightly on both sides, then add the sausages and their fat to the beans in the casserole and stir in gently.

Remove all the meat from the gammon or ham bone and chop into chunks. Carve the salt pork into thick slices and then into chunks. Return the meat to the casserole; simmer for a few minutes, check the seasonings and serve. The dish is distinctly spicy, so fresh green cabbage is the ideal accompaniment, with a fruity red wine.

Since most Spanish wine is blended, different styles of wine are identified with brand names. The biggest *bodega* in Rioja is Campo Viejo, and their big seller in Spain is San Ascensio *2° año sin crianza* wine, which means 'two years old and not aged in wood'. Another household brand of young red Rioja is Banda Azul *3° año* – Ernest Hemingway's favourite wine – from Frederick Paternina, the largest exporter.

EMPANADA DE RAXÓ

GALICIAN PORK AND SAUSAGE PIE

Pies are a feature of Galicia: fish pies baked on the shore for the returning fishermen, with scallops, or cockles and sweetcorn, or meat pies, like this one, with *chorizos* in the filling. *Raxó* is dialect for 'pork loin' and this pie is the equivalent of *lasagne*, a cheap and good-tempered dish for a crowd.

SERVES 8

PORK FILLING
1 kg (2 lb) boned loin of pork, cubed then diced
3 cooking chorizos or other fresh spicy sausage
175 g (6 oz) raw ham or smoked gammon, diced
250 (8 oz) onions, chopped
4 garlic cloves, finely chopped
500 g (1 lb) mixed peppers, seeded and chopped
200 g (7 oz) canned tomatoes, with juice
2 hard-boiled eggs, chopped
1 g packet of saffron
1 teaspoon paprika
2 tablespoons chopped parsley
125 – 150 ml (4 – 5 fl oz) olive oil
175 ml (6 fl oz) dry white wine
salt and freshly ground black pepper

WINE PASTRY
400 g (14 oz) flour, plus extra for sprinkling
75 g (3 oz) lard or margarine
75 ml (3 fl oz) olive oil
3 small eggs, 1 of them beaten for glazing
50 ml (2 fl oz) dry white wine
1 teaspoon salt

Make the filling in advance. Fry the onions in 125 ml (4 fl oz) oil over medium heat, adding the garlic when they begin to colour. Add the pork and ham or gammon and fry until coloured, stirring regularly. Add 2 more tablespoons of oil if necessary, and add the chopped *chorizo* and peppers. Fry gently.

Add the tomatoes, wine, saffron, paprika and parsley and season generously. Cook gently for 20 minutes until the pork is done and the liquid has evaporated and thickened. Leave to cool.

Make the wine pastry. Use a food processor to work the fat into the flour-plus-salt, then the oil, wine and 2 eggs. Alternatively, make a well in the middle of the flour, melt the flat and pour it into the middle then work everything in gradually with your fingers. Blend to a smooth pastry and chill for 15 – 20 minutes.

Heat the oven with a baking tray to 190° C (375° F, gas 5). Choose a small roasting tin or large rectangular ovenproof dish, between 30 × 20 cm (12 × 8 in) and 28 cm (11 in) square. This is a handy pie, as there is no problem if the container is too big, because of the way the pastry folds.

Divide the pastry in half, then pull off a knob (small egg size) and add it to the base pastry. Roll out the bottom layer thinly, so it is large enough to just hang over the container sides. Lift it, rolled round the rolling pin, and press gently into the container. Smooth the cold filling into the pie and sprinkle with the chopped egg.

Trim off overhanging pastry, to just below the rim on the outside of the container, then fold it inwards over the meat and brush the turnover with egg. Roll out the lid and place on top. Press the two together all round with a fork: this is characteristic of the pie. Brush with more egg and prick the surface. Bake on the hot tray for 40 minutes. Cabbage goes well with the pie, freshly boiled, or part-cooked then fried with garlic, and, to accompany it, any expansive fruity red wine. Ribera del Duero comes from northern Spain, but there is a wide choice of regional Spanish wine, simply labelled *reserva*.

EMPANADA DE RAXÓ *top*, POLLO EN CHILINDRÓN *bottom* (*p 110*).

POLLO EN CHILINDRÓN

CHICKEN WITH RED PEPPER, HAM AND TOMATOES

Aragon is sometimes described as the 'zone of *chilindrónes*', so popular is this dish, which is also made with lamb and pork. In *Viaje por La Cocina Española*, Luis Antonio de Vega describes a custom, dating back to Moorish times, for workmen joining a workshop to treat their mates to this dish. Later on it was eaten to seal a bargain – and referred to as 'the tip'.

SERVES 4

1.5 kg (3¼ lb) chicken, preferably corn-fed, quartered and backbone removed
200 g (7 oz) smoked gammon or raw ham, diced
1 onion, chopped
2 garlic cloves, finely chopped
3 red peppers, chopped
75 g (3 oz) canned tomatoes, drained
¼ dried chilli, seeded and chopped
2 tablespoons olive oil
2 teaspoons paprika
salt and freshly ground black pepper

Remove the wing tips and rub salt and paprika into the chicken portions. Heat the oil in a casserole into which the chicken will fit comfortably and put in the chicken portions, skin-side down. Fry over medium-low heat, turning until golden on all sides.

While the chicken is cooking, distribute the onion and diced ham in the gaps in the casserole and fry, stirring every now and then, until soft. Corn-fed chicken gives off its fat, so you may be able to remove a couple of spoonfuls of oil at this point. Conversely, other birds may need a little more oil adding.

Pour boiling water over the chopped red pepper and soak for 10 minutes. Drain well, then blot on paper. If you have a food processor, pulse briefly (this is not crucial, however).

If the pan is very full, you may find it easier to take out the chicken briefly. Add the garlic, peppers and chopped tomato to the pan, with the dried chilli. Cook and let it reduce for 4–5 minutes, check salt and pepper then cook covered (with the chicken) for 10 minutes. Small new potatoes go well with this.

Quintessentially Spanish, and no worse for being a working-class dish, this chicken calls for a red wine that is unmistakably from the same country, with a hint of the oak cask about it – a characteristic all Riojas share. *Reservas* are a minimum of four years old, with one year at least in the barrel (and often more), well-balanced wines, with a satisfying long aftertaste. Try a Viña Herminia Lagunilla *reserva*, 2 years in the barrel, or the fresh, lighter Viña Albina *reserva*.

STREET IN MADRID *A solitary lamppost casts its shadow in the baking heat of the midday sun.*

MEADOW IN EXTREMADURA (overleaf) *A carpet of purple clover puts on a dazzling display.*

PEPITORIA DE GALLINA

CHICKEN FRICASSEE WITH ALMOND SAUCE

A *pepita* is a pip – pine-nuts, sunflower seeds, even melon seeds and tomato pips are all covered by the word – though almonds are now used in this dish rather than the original pine-nuts. The dish is Moorish and dates back at least to the 13th century. A *gallina* is a hen, and I guess it was a tough one, for the old recipe stewed it for a long time in stock, which was then thickened with hard-boiled egg yolks as well as the almonds which are used in the modern recipe.

SERVES 4

1.25–1.3 kg (2¾–3 lb) free-range or corn-fed chicken, cut up (see page 22), without wing tips
25 blanched almonds
1 g packet of saffron powder or 5 saffron strands
2 garlic cloves, finely chopped
1 thick slice bread, without crusts
1 tablespoon parsley, chopped so finely 'it becomes invisible'
about 50 ml (2 fl oz) olive oil
125 ml (4 fl oz) good chicken stock
125 ml (4 fl oz) pale dry Montilla wine or fino sherry
1 bay leaf, crumbled
4 sprigs of fresh thyme
tiny pinch of freshly grated nutmeg
tiny pinch of powdered clove
salt and freshly ground black pepper
1 teaspoon lemon juice

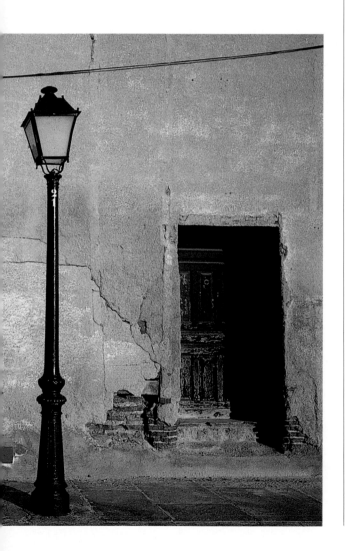

Start the sauce. Toast the almonds in a low oven (about 150°C [300°F, gas 2]) shaking the pan occasionally, until they are biscuit-coloured and give off a pleasant smell. If using saffron powder, toast the paper packet in the same pan until the paper just colours.

Heat the oil in a wide shallow casserole, frying the garlic and removing it before the oil gets too hot. Over high heat fry the bread quickly on both sides then reserve it with the garlic.

Season the chicken pieces well and fry them in the casserole, turning till golden on all sides – about 20 minutes. A free-range chicken may need more oil, but a corn-fed one will give it off.

Remove the chicken from the pan and drain off any excess oil. Dissolve the saffron in a cup with 2 tablespoons of hot stock, then add the remaining stock, with the Montilla, to the pan, stirring to deglaze the bottom. Return the chicken to the pan, add the bay leaf and thyme and cover. Cook gently for 10 minutes.

Make the sauce: grind the toasted almonds in a small blender, then add the bread in pieces, garlic, parsley, saffron liquid, nutmeg and clove and reduce to an aromatic purée. Stir this into the chicken juices, with the lemon juice, and serve. Crisp mange-tout make a fresh accompaniment.

PERDIZ EN CHOCOLATE

PARTRIDGE WITH CHOCOLATE SAUCE

Partridge is almost an everyday dish in many rural families, by far and away the most popular of game birds in Spain. The red-legged (or French) partridge is native to southwest Europe and, once trapped, the birds are often kept ready to hand in cages hanging outside the house. Four pigeons can be substituted, but in this case use about 150 ml ($\frac{1}{4}$ pt) extra stock.

Chocolate is quite common in game sauces all over Spain, particularly with rabbit. It gives the sauce a deliciously subtle flavour for, of course, it is not naturally sweet. This dish comes from Valladolid in Castile, but similar dishes are cooked all along the Pyrenees. In Catalonia chocolate sauce is even served with lobster.

SERVES 4

2 partridges, cleaned
1 onion, chopped
3 garlic cloves, finely chopped
8 shallots or pickling onions
3 carrots, in short lengths
3 tablespoons pork fat or olive oil
about 2 tablespoons flour
2 tablespoons Spanish brandy
250 ml (8 fl oz) red wine
250 ml (8 fl oz) good chicken stock
4 tablespoons wine vinegar
6 peppercorns
2 cloves
1 bay leaf
25 g (1 oz) dark chocolate, grated
salt and freshly ground black pepper

Reach into the neck of the bird, run finger and thumb nails up the wishbone to the top and pull it out. Halve the birds, cutting on both sides of the backbone and on one side of the breast bone. Blot inside with kitchen paper. Rub the birds with brandy, salt and pepper then let them sit for 30 minutes.

Heat the fat or oil in a casserole into which the birds will fit snugly, and fry the onion gently, adding the garlic as it softens. Sprinkle the birds lightly with flour

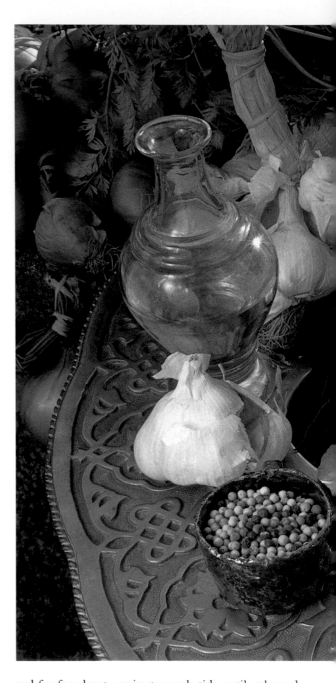

and fry for about 5 minutes each side until coloured.

Pour in the wine and stock and add the vinegar, peppercorns, cloves and bay leaf. Bring to simmering point, then cover and cook very gently for 40 minutes. Add the pickling onions, if using, then 5 minutes later the carrots; shallots should go in with the carrots. Simmer for another 15 minutes.

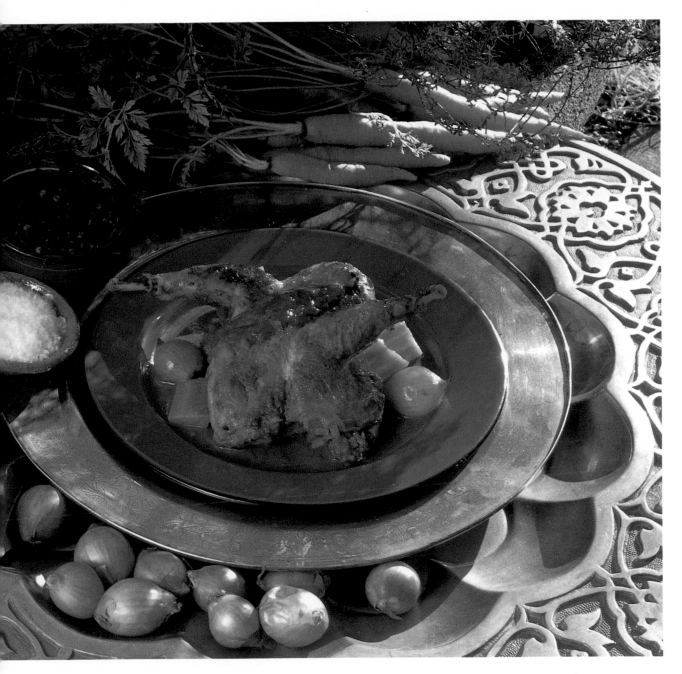

Spoon the birds and vegetables from the pan. Reduce the sauce by boiling if there is more than about 300–350 ml (10–12 fl oz), then purée in a blender. Return to the pan and add the chocolate, stirring until it is dissolved. Arrange the partridges and vegetables back in the casserole, spooning a little sauce over them. Serve with a good Rioja *reserva*.

PERDIZ EN CHOCOLATE

115

PATO CON HIGOS

ROAST DUCK WITH DRIED FIGS

Ducks and figs have been linked for centuries – the birds love to feed on the half-ripe fruit that never matures. The Romans were the first to discover the beneficial effect that figs had on the duck's liver. It seems appropriate, therefore, to make this Pyrenean dish with a grey Barbary duck, the type traditionally used for fattening livers for *foie gras*. These birds have started appearing in supermarkets and have gamey flesh and far less fat than white ducks.

Dried figs have a beautiful affinity with *amontillado*

sherry and the sauce is just lifted from sweetness by the lemon oil in the fresh zest, added at the last moment. Bunches of dressed watercress will add colour.

SERVES 4

1.8 kg (4 lb) oven-ready duckling, or 1.5 kg (3¼ lb)
Barbary duck
300 g (10 oz) ready-to-eat dried figs
2 tablespoons pork fat or butter
1 onion, finely chopped
2 garlic cloves, finely chopped
250 ml (8 fl oz) giblet or chicken stock
250 ml (8 fl oz) amontillado or dry oloroso sherry
grated zest of ½ lemon
salt and freshly ground black pepper

Heat the oven; if using a white duck, to 200° C (400° F, gas 6), if using a Barbary duck, to 220° C (425° F, gas 7). Prick the duck fat all over and season the bird inside and out. Melt the pork fat or butter in a roasting tin into which the duck just fits and put it in, breast down. Cook on top of the stove, turning it over and propping against the edge, until coloured on all sides. Drain and reserve the fat and put the duck in the oven to roast – for about 1¼ hours for a duck at the lower temperature, 35–40 minutes for a Barbary duck.

Meanwhile use 2 tablespoons of the duck fat to sweat the onions in a saucepan until soft, adding the garlic towards the end. Add the stock and let it reduce and concentrate. In another pan simmer the figs in the sherry for 10 minutes. Then drain as much fat as you can from the roasting tin and baste the duck with 125 ml (4 fl oz) of the fig juice.

Reserve 8 figs for a garnish and purée the remaining figs and juice with the stock and onion in a blender. Return to the pan.

Remove the duck to a warm serving plate to rest. Strain off the fat from the roasting tin and add the juices to the sauce. Add the lemon zest and check the seasoning. Quarter the duck and serve garnished with figs and accompanied by the sauce. With it serve a red wine from the Rioja Alta, such as a Viña Ardanza *reserva*, an unmistakably Spanish wine with an immediate oaky aroma and often a rich, creamy vanilla taste, that it is almost like a pudding.

CODORNICES ASADAS CON AJOS

ROAST QUAIL WITH GARLIC CLOVES

Quails are wild birds in Spain, trapped by nets as they fly through the mountain passes during migration twice a year. You might find this simple country dish in any small *venta* or roadside eatery, usually served with

FLOCK OF SHEEP IN ZAMORA *The exquisite roast lamb of Castile is highly regarded throughout Spain.*

mounds of chips, though *patatas picantes* (see page 71) are good too.

Other small birds can be roasted the same way: for 2 partridges allow 30–35 minutes, or roast a single guinea fowl for 40–45 minutes, turning it 3 times.

SERVES 4

*8 small quail
75 ml (3 fl oz) olive oil
24 garlic cloves
4 tablespoons red wine or sweet Malaga wine
flour
salt and freshly ground black pepper*

To prepare the quail, snip off the wings at the joint, if they are still there, then reach into the quail's neck and find the wishbone on each side with your thumb and index finger. Run your nails up to the top of the wishbone and pinch it out. It is then possible to eat the cooked birds neatly with a knife and fork.

Cut across the stem end of the garlic cloves with a big kitchen knife, then lay the flat of the knife on them in turn and press. This pops off the skin and crushes them. Put a small clove into each quail and salt and pepper the birds.

Heat the oven to 220° C (425° F, gas 7) with a roasting tin containing the oil and the remaining crushed garlic cloves. Put in the birds breast down (this saves all the business of barding them with bacon) and roast for 10 minutes. Turn them over, basting them well, and shake the merest dusting of flour through a sieve on to the breasts. Add the wine to the pan and cook for another 10–15 minutes, when they will be crispy on top.

Move the birds to a serving platter, garnishing them with the garlic cloves, which are now quite mild, and spoon off all the oil from the pan. Serve 2 quails per person, with a spoonful of pan juices.

Our farmed quail taste less of game than wild birds, so try a light but balanced fruity red Senoria de Los Llanos *Gran Reserva* from Valdepeñas. With partridges or guinea fowl, however, a bottle of Torres Gran Sangredetoro, which is full-bodied and fruity, would show to advantage. It is one of the few Penedès wines made from native grapes and still typical of wine produced in the region in times past.

ESCABECHE DE PERDICES

SOUSED PARTRIDGES

The Arabs invented pickling in vinegar as a means of keeping cooked meat fresh – the word *escabeche* comes from the Persian *sikbāj*, 'acid food'. In Spain, however, the method was enthusiastically adopted for fish. It then travelled inland, and has become a speciality for game birds and rabbit in Old Castile.

A convenient party food, I was once served this old-fashioned dish with a *nouvelle cuisine* garnish, which suited it well.

SERVES 4

2 partridges, cleaned
1 small onion, chopped
1 celery stalk, diced small
4 garlic cloves, finely chopped
2 tablespoons olive oil
175 ml (6 fl oz) dry white wine
175 ml (6 fl oz) tarragon vinegar
175 ml (6 fl oz) chicken stock
2 cloves
1 bay leaf
2 sprigs fresh thyme or a pinch of dried thyme
salt and freshly ground black pepper
4 carrots
½ lettuce

Reach into the neck of the bird and run finger and thumb nails up the wishbone to the top and pull it out. Salt and pepper the birds. Choose a saucepan into which they fit snugly side by side. Heat the oil in the pan and fry the birds, turning them over and propping them against the sides of the pan, until they are coloured on all sides. Remove the birds.

Fry the onion in the same pan until soft, adding the chopped celery and then the garlic when the onion starts to soften. Pull the vegetables to the sides of the pan and put in the birds, packing the pan tightly. Add the wine, vinegar, stock, cloves, bay leaf and thyme and bring gently to the boil. Simmer for 1 hour, adding water to keep the birds covered. Transfer the partridges to a 15 cm (6 in) diameter dish (without using your fingers). They should be packed in tightly and completely covered with the stock, when this is poured

in. The stock will jelly round the birds, which will keep for a week.

To serve, split the birds in 2, cutting out the backbones. Arrange in a dish with a little jellied stock (melting it and glazing the birds, if you wish). Make the garnish. For carrot 'flowers', make grooves lengthways down the carrot on all sides with a canelle cutter or fork, then cut in rounds and cook briefly. Roll some lettuce leaves in wads, then cut across to make ribbons. Arrange round the birds.

A Navarra red would go well with the cold birds. This district adjoins Rioja and shares many of its wine characteristics. What these wines lack in finesse they make up for in fresh fruitiness – needed here to balance the vinegar.

CONEJO GUISADO A LA BURGALESA

STEWED RABBIT FROM BURGOS

Most regions of Spain have their own recipes for rabbit: with garlic in La Mancha, with rosemary in Catalonia. Rabbits are frequently cooked with another free food – snails – which feed on rosemary and therefore act as a walking *bouquet garni*. Serve this stew from the heart of Old Castile with boiled carrots or fried mushrooms with thyme.

SERVES 6

2.25 kg (5 lb) rabbit (or 2 small ones), giving 1.3 kg
(3 lb) meat, in 6 serving portions
1 rabbit liver (or turkey liver)
50 g (2 oz) pork fat or 4 tablespoons olive oil
2 onions, chopped
4 garlic cloves, finely chopped
1 celery stalk, chopped
2 ripe tomatoes, without skin or seeds, chopped
1 bay leaf
1 sprig thyme
175 ml (6 fl oz) white wine
300 ml (10 fl oz) chicken stock
grating of fresh nutmeg
salt and freshly ground black pepper
chopped parsley to garnish

With 4 legs and the saddle split lengthways, a rabbit makes 6 portions. Season the meat and heat the fat or oil in a shallow casserole in which the rabbit will fit in one layer. Fry the hind legs for 5 minutes, turning, then add the remaining portions and cook until golden on all sides. Remove the meat then fry the liver for 2 minutes each side and reserve it. Add the onion to the pan with the celery and cook until softened, adding the garlic towards the end. Return the rabbit to the pan and add the wine, stock, crushed tomato, bay leaf and thyme. Grate a tiny amount of nutmeg over the top. Simmer, covered, for 45 minutes for tender rabbit (imported, tough Chinese rabbit can take $1\frac{1}{2}$ hours).

Remove the rabbit to a serving dish. Purée the liver in a blender and stir into the sauce to thicken it. Check the seasonings, including the nutmeg, then spoon over the rabbit. Sprinkle with a little parsley. Rabbit never divides into fair portions – the hind legs have most meat and the saddle is good for those who hate bones.

VENADO ASADO CON SALSA DE CABRALES

ROAST VENISON WITH BLUE CHEESE SAUCE

There are still bears and wolves in the mountains of the Picos de Europa in northern Spain, one of the largest wild areas in Europe. Chamois and deer run here in considerable numbers.

The region also produces Spain's most delicious cheese, Cabrales. Moist and blue, matured in caves with stalactites and sent to market wrapped in plane leaves, it is similar to Roquefort. I have eaten this same sauce made with Roquefort, in a different range of Spanish mountains, the Pyrenees, where Roquefort is a local ingredient. On that occasion it was served with boned, rolled, roast pork loin.

SERVES 6

700 g (1½ lb) venison loin, or 1.1 kg (2½ lb) haunch or leg, sold rolled, tied and barded with pork fat
500 ml (16 fl oz) red wine (for leg)
3–4 tablespoons butter or pork fat
salt and freshly ground black pepper

BLUE CHEESE SAUCE
2 tablespoons Fundador or another Spanish brandy
250 ml (8 fl oz) whipping cream
75 g (3 oz) Cabrales or Roquefort cheese

A loin of venison roasts like a beef fillet – it is more expensive, but wonderfully tender and less meat is needed, because the long thin shape makes neat slices. A joint from the top of the leg is more like beef topside – a wider joint, slightly coarser and more likely to shrink in the oven; more is needed. Leg is often sold with a covering of pork fat, to prevent it drying out during roasting. It is also tougher and so it is wise to marinate it beforehand. Remove the barding and string, put the leg in a small but deep bowl, pour the wine over and leave for 24 hours, turning once.

Heat the oven to 200° C (400° F, gas 6). Season the venison. Melt the butter or fat in a small roasting tin, put in the venison and turn it to seal all sides. Move to the oven and roast a loin for 25 minutes and a leg roll (retied, with the barding fat back in place) for 50 minutes, basting the meat at least once. Let the joint rest on a warm serving platter.

Spoon off the fat from the roasting tin, if the meat was barded. Put it over low heat and add the brandy, stirring to pick up the juices. Add the cream and boil to reduce a little. Mash in the crumbled cheese with a spoon. Carve a loin into 6 uniform slices and serve on a platter. Carve the rolled leg at table, and serve the sauce separately in a sauce boat.

With this drink a local wine, like Vega de Toro *tinto reserva*. Full-bodied, deep in colour with something of blackcurrant about it, this wine comes from the newest of Spain's *appellation contrôlée* districts, although Toro is reputedly the oldest red wine in Spain. It went with Columbus to America and has been called the 'thinking wine', because it has been patronized by the University of Salamanca since the 13th century.

MORTERUELO

HARE, CHICKEN, HAM AND LIVER TERRINE

Don Quixote ate this peasant dish at El Toboso in La Mancha, nearly 400 years ago. It's a typical mixture of game and the cheaper meats from the farm: *gazpacho manchego* has the same mixture. Only the bony front part of the hare is included, reserving the prime meat of the saddle and back legs for roasting.

The classic method is to pulverize everything together in a mortar – which gives the hash its name – and serve it hot. But with three such different meats I prefer to shred them and serve the dish cold as an unusually seasoned, coarse-textured pâté.

SERVES 12 – 15

2 hare front legs and rib cage, about 550 g (1¼ lb)
½ chicken, about 700 g (1½ lb) including backbone
400 g (14 oz) smoked gammon
550 g (1¼ lb) lamb's liver, trimmed and cubed
1 pig's trotter, split
500 g (1 lb) pork back fat, cubed
750 ml (1¼ pt) dry white wine
2 onions, finely chopped
6 garlic cloves, finely chopped
6 tablespoons chopped parsley
2 teaspoons paprika
¼ teaspoon ground cinnamon
½ teaspoon ground cumin
⅛ teaspoon ground clove
2 teaspoons salt
freshly ground black pepper
50 g (2 oz) breadcrumbs
50 g (2 oz) walnuts, coarsely chopped

Put the gammon in a saucepan, cover with cold water and bring to the boil. Simmer for 5 minutes then drain. Split the hare legs from the rib cage and pack the hare, chicken, gammon and trotter into a pan. Cover with the wine and simmer for 40 minutes.

SHUTTERED HOUSE *With its lowered shutters and sleepy air, the house, as well as its inhabitants, seems to be enjoying a* siesta.

Chop the pork fat and heat in a frying pan until it gives off its fat: pour into a heat-proof jug until there is 250 ml (8 fl oz). Discard the bits from the pan, then use some fat from the jug to fry the onion gently until softened, adding the garlic towards the end. Turn the onion into a food processor, or better still a blender.

When the chicken will come easily off the bone, remove it to a well-scrubbed board and pick all the meat off it with two forks (no fingers should be used from now on as the dish is to be kept). Pick the meat into shreds and transfer to a shallow serving bowl about 2.4 l (4 pt) capacity. Return the bones and skin to the pan and continue simmering. Transfer the gammon to the board and remove the rind and fat. Break up the meat into shreds and add to the chicken in the bowl.

Heat more fat in the frying pan and fry the liver in 3 batches over high heat, sprinkling it with salt and plenty of freshly ground pepper. Add the liver to the onions in the blender when cooked. Reduce them to a purée, adding the paprika, cinnamon, cumin and clove. Heat all but about 3 tablespoons of the remaining fat in the frying pan and return the liver purée to the heat and fry it gently.

Pick the hare meat off the bones and add to the bowl. Discard the trotter, strain the juices from the pan and add to the liver. Then stir in the parsley with the breadcrumbs and walnuts to stiffen the hash. Finally add all the shredded meat and check the seasoning. Traditionally this is served hot. To serve cold, pack into the serving bowl, smoothing the top with the back of a spoon. Warm the remaining fat and spoon it over the top, chill and leave to mature for 48 hours. Serve with French bread.

DESSERTS AND DRINKS

Spain is blessed with a mouthwatering abundance of fresh fruit and a dessert-making tradition of depth and subtlety, in which Moorish influences are unmistakable.

FRESAS CON ANIS *left (p 138)*, MANTECADOS *right (p 134)*.

THE GRAPES WERE 'as big as plums, the melons melted on the tongue like snow, the wine was fiery and potent' raved Hans Christian Anderson, visiting Valencia in the 1860s. With apples in the Pyrenees, peach orchards in Navarre, melons in Lérida, pomegranates named after Granada, plums drying for Christmas alongside the chillies in Rioja and muscatel grapes on the hot coasts of Valencia and Alicante, Spain claims the best fruit in the world, and appropriately fruit ends most Spanish meals.

Oranges are almost the symbol of Spain, introduced by the Moors a couple of centuries before the Crusaders took them to Sicily and Italy. Our so-called 'Sevilles' were planted in the beautiful courtyards of the Alhambra in Granada and throughout the south. With them came lemons and the forerunner of the grapefruit. Sweet oranges came in the 15th century.

At almost all other times of the day, apart from *postre*, 'afters', the Spanish sweet tooth is gratified by a range of dessert wines and liqueurs and special-occasion sweets, some of almost Oriental sugariness. Almonds and honey are included in many of them. *Turrón*, or nougat, white or dark, soft or brittle, is exceedingly more-ish and is now a big industry in Jijona. The Arabic influences in sweet-making are pronounced and sweets such as *amaguillos* date from Moorish times.

They might shy away from the idea, but the nuns of innumerable orders are the direct successors to the Moors, as sweetmakers. The reason is that egg whites are used to clarify sherry and even red wine, and the yolks have then traditionally been given away for charity. From them the nuns created specialities to sell, sometimes their only source of income. *Yemas*, meaning 'yolks', are combined with sugar and the names of the sweets come from their shape, like *rosquillas*, rings, or from the order which cherishes the recipe, like San Leandro in Seville or Santa Teresa in Avila.

In the Spanish kitchen, milk and cream are commandeered for desserts, particularly in the north. Curds and junket, *cuajarda*, are served with spoonfuls of honey and cold rice milk pudding, *arroz con leche,* is popular. Much richer sweets are made from custard, often fried in squares as *leche frita*. Chilled *natilla*, a custard deeply flavoured with cinnamon and lemon zest, is found all over Spain. The national dessert, however, is caramel custard, called *flan*. A blissful southern version, made with syrup rather than milk, is called *tocino de cielo* – 'heavenly bacon', which is exactly how it looks.

Ices have a 1000-year history in Spain, for even the south has high mountains, and in the 19th century Washington Irving noted the snow-gatherers working at night in the Sierra Nevada, to rush ice to Granada before dawn. The favourite ice creams are delicious lemon sorbets packed into their own shells and cinnamon ice cream, which is preferred to vanilla.

The Spanish discoveries in the Americas changed Spanish desserts by making sugar cheap, and establishing 'burnt' sugar as a very Spanish taste. With sugar came chocolate, used originally for drinks but not sweets, and a Spanish monopoly for over a century. More important, the association of chocolate with cinnamon began and this persists in Spain, though vanilla has long since taken over elsewhere. Curiously, the *conquistadores* missed the vanilla bean entirely.

Rich, sweet little biscuits hold pride of place in the festival kitchen. All over Spain you may find *polvorones, mantecados y almendrados* – crumble cakes, lardy cakes or almond biscuits – which are ideal companions to wine. Pine-nuts go into *piñonates* and *mostachónes*, S-shaped biscuits which make 'moustaches' in pairs.

Little choux puffs like *buñuelos* are made for Saints' days, particularly for that of San Isidro, the patron saint of Madrid, and deep-fried and stuffed *huesos de santo*, saint's bones, are made for All Saints on 1st November, though these are becoming harder to find. The marzipan *figuritas* of Toledo are eaten everywhere at Christmas. Spaniards are also fond of sweet pastries, like the ground almond *tarta de Santiago*, found on many tables on St James' day, topped with a stencil of St James' big sword in powdered sugar.

From Moorish times drinks were offered with sweets as a gesture of hospitality. Spanish brandy is perfumed and sweet and there is a fondness for sweet alcohols like anis. The day may start with a sweet, thick chocolate drink, while *horchata*, a milk made from tigernuts and sometimes iced, suits the morning or late afternoon. Hot weather brings *leche merengada*, chilled milk with meringue, on to café menus. There are also long drinks of wines with citrus juice, like *sangría*, and the less-known Basque punch, *linoyada*, with red and white wines. And for the night, there are regional punches, like *queimada*, which can blow your legs away.

CREMA CATALANA

BURNT CATALAN CREAM

The Catalans claim to have invented grilled sugar, and this classic custard, with its Middle Eastern flavours of cinnamon and lemon, justifies the name of 'burnt cream' far better than *crème brûlée*. The caramel forms the merest net on top and it tastes delicately grilled rather than of toffee. The sugar is traditionally caramelized with a salamander, a round branding iron, about 5 cm (2 in) across, on a long handle, which is heated to red-hot. These are sometimes sold in smart kitchen shops abroad.

The easiest and neatest way of all to caramelize sugar, however, is with a small butane gas torch (of the type used for paint-stripping). This way a fine layer of brittle caramel is possible. Domestic grills rarely get hot enough to grill the sugar quickly, so a thick, impervious layer is needed to protect the custard.

SERVES 6

250 ml (8 fl oz) milk
250 ml (8 fl oz) single cream
4 large egg yolks
1 tablespoon cornflour
75 g (3 oz) sugar
4 strips of lemon zest
1 cinnamon stick
4 tablespoons Demerara sugar for grilling

Heat the milk and cream with the lemon zest and cinnamon stick to simmering point, then leave the pan off the heat, to infuse for 20 minutes. Beat together the egg yolks, cornflour and sugar with a wooden spoon until light and fluffy.

Fish the cinnamon and lemon zest out of the milk, bring gently back to a simmer and pour on to the yolks. Return the mixture to the saucepan and stir gently over low heat. Mercifully this custard doesn't need a double boiler, because the cornflour prevents any risk of curdling. When the custard will coat the spoon, pour it into 6 tiny earthenware dishes, or small ramekins, and chill.

About 30 minutes before serving, sprinkle the Demerara sugar lightly over the top of each one and then give them 15 – 20 seconds of intense heat – a low blast from the butane torch. (The caramel melts in the custard, if done too far ahead.) You can try grilling these under the hottest part of your grill, but I can't promise this will be successful. They are also good plain and served very cold. Return to the refrigerator until ready to serve. The cream is luscious with a chilled glass of Bach Extrésimo *blanco semi dulce*. This is not a Muscat wine and is surprisingly refreshing for a sweet Spanish white, with a drop of honey in the finish.

MARQUESA DE CHOCOLATE VALENCIANA

VALENCIA CHOCOLATE MOUSSE

Unusually for a Spanish dessert, this chocolate mousse is not sweet. Yet it is the lightest, most chocolatey pudding in the world.

SERVES 6

100 g (4 oz) best-quality chocolate, broken into small pieces
3 tablespoons cocoa powder (unsweetened)
50 g (2 oz) unsalted butter, diced
2 large egg yolks
3 large egg whites
2 tablespoons caster sugar
chopped crystallized orange peel to decorate

Melt the chocolate carefully in a bowl over barely simmering water, stirring and making sure the bottom doesn't cook. Stir in the cocoa powder. Remove from the heat and beat in the butter until smooth.

Separate the eggs, stirring 2 yolks into the chocolate mixture. Whisk the 3 egg whites to soft peaks. Sprinkle the sugar over the whites and whisk for 2 – 3 minutes to make a glossy meringue. Spoon the chocolate over the top in 2 – 3 batches and fold in with a big spoon, cutting it down into the meringue with the spoon edge.

Spoon into 6 small ramekins, 75 ml (3 fl oz) size, or small straight-sided wine glasses. Decorate the tops with a little chopped crystallized orange peel and chill until needed. Malaga *dulce*, the golden Mountain wine, goes perfectly with it.

FLAN DE NARANJA

ORANGE CARAMEL CREAMS

If Spain has a national pudding, it is *flan*: a delicate little castle of custard, topped with melted caramel, and nothing to do with pastry. This Valencian version is made with orange juice rather than milk, a few sweet spoonfuls only, and with its beautiful texture is perfect to end a meal.

SERVES 6

7 large egg yolks
1 large egg
250 g (9 oz) caster sugar
2–3 large oranges, 200 ml (7 fl oz) juice

Heat the oven to 170° C (325° F, gas 3) and arrange 6 dariole moulds, 100 ml (3½ fl oz) size, or *demi-tasse* coffee cups (not valuable ones), in a small roasting tin.

Put 50 g (2 oz) sugar in a small pan with 2 tablespoons of water for the caramel and heat gently, stirring to dissolve the sugar. Let it boil until it turns light brown and smells of caramel, then remove it immediately from the heat. Quickly pour about 1 tablespoonful into the bottom of each mould or cup, turning it to coat the bottom and a little of the sides.

Grate the zest from 1 orange on your finest grater, then use a little of the remaining sugar to mop up the shreds and the orange oil from the grater. Put the yolks and whole egg in a bowl and beat lightly with a wooden spoon to combine them. Bring the orange juice and sugar to boiling point, stirring to dissolve the sugar, then turn down the heat and boil for 2 minutes.

Pour the hot juice on to the yolks, stirring, then pass through a sieve. Divide the mixture between the dariole moulds in the tin (they won't be quite full). Pour boiling water round them, to come two-thirds of the way up the sides of the moulds. Bake for 30 minutes, remove the tin from the oven and leave the dariole moulds in the water until cool enough to handle, then chill. Serve turned out, with a little of their caramel syrup spooned round them.

TARTA QUEMADA HELADA

ORANGE ICE CREAM WITH BRITTLE CARAMEL

The Spaniards are extremely fond of ice creams, which are sold everywhere but less often made at home. This combination of luscious orange-studded ice cream and crisp caramel is absolutely stunning.

A *tarta* simply means a 'dessert' and, like so many others in Andalusia, this one contains numerous egg yolks as these are a by-product of sherry-making.

SERVES 8

300 ml (½ pt) double cream
300 ml (½ pt) milk, hot
8 large egg yolks
125 g (4 oz) caster sugar
50 g (2 oz) chopped crystallized orange peel
1 tablespoon Grand Marnier or Triple Sec (optional)
1 teaspoon vanilla extract
about 250 g (8 oz) Demerara sugar

Soak the peel in the orange liqueur if it seems hard. Whisk the yolks and caster sugar until creamy in a bowl which fits over a pan of simmering water. Pour the hot milk on to the yolks, add the vanilla and stir until the custard is thick – the bowl must not touch the water. Press a butter paper or piece of cling film down on the surface of the custard to prevent a skin forming, and leave till cold.

Whisk the cream until thick, then fold in the orange peel and liqueur. Fold the cream into the custard. Spoon into 8 ramekins or small shallow baking dishes, no more than three-quarters full, and chill, then freeze until firm.

Heat the grill until very hot. Spread about 2 tablespoons of Demerara sugar over the top of each dish and grill under the hottest spot, in batches if necessary, until caramelized – up to 2 minutes. Remove the ramekins to cool in a sink in a little cold water, then chill and return to the freezer for about 3 hours.

Allow the *tartas* 30 minutes out of the freezer in the fridge before serving, to soften slightly. The caramel top will be brittle and the ice cream is so rich it should be eaten slowly, ideally with a glass of Freixenet, the popular Spanish *champán*.

TARTA AL WHISKY

FROZEN WHISKY LAYER CAKE

From Galicia in the north across the country to the Mediterranean in the south, most restaurants offer this ice cream cake. It is made by all the big ice cream manufacturers and is favoured for Sunday lunch out, which in Spain is a family affair. It can be delicious or indifferent – like Black Forest gâteau in southern Germany which suffers the same fate. Home-made, it is genuinely good. It's a clever ice too, because it has two layers of different vanilla ice creams, one incorporating the egg yolks, the other made with the egg whites.

SERVES 12

sponge cake recipe (see page 133)
4 tablespoons whisky

GOLDEN VANILLA ICE CREAM
450 ml (16 fl oz) milk
250 ml (8 fl oz) whipping cream
6 large egg yolks
75 g (3 oz) caster sugar
1 teaspoon vanilla extract
4 tablespoons whisky
4 tablespoons praline (see recipe below)

WHITE VANILLA ICE CREAM
4 egg whites
125 g (4 oz) caster sugar
250 ml (8 fl oz) whipping cream
1 teaspoon vanilla extract

PRALINE, CARAMEL AND DECORATION
100 g (4 oz) almonds
50 g (2 oz) hazelnuts
275 g (9 oz) caster sugar
125 ml (4 fl oz) whipping cream

Make the cake mixture and bake it in a 24 cm (9 ½ in) spring-release cake tin at 180° C (350° F, gas 4) for 15 minutes. Cool on a wire rack.

Make the praline. Heat 115 g (4 oz) sugar with 2 tablespoons of water in a saucepan until caramelized to a light brown. Add the nuts, stir for 1 minute, then turn out on to greased foil. When cold (quite soon), break up the sheet of nuts and caramel, and chop coarsely. Chop a good 4 tablespoons more finely, and reserve these for flavouring the golden ice cream.

Use the same pan to make the caramel for the top of the cake. Cover a flat baking sheet with foil and draw round the cake tin with a ball-point pen. Make the caramel as before, and pour into the circle. Spread with the back of the spoon, keeping just inside the line. Immediately mark the disc across with a long knife, dipped in hot water to make 12 portions.

Make the golden vanilla ice cream. Prepare a double boiler with a little simmering water in the bottom. Cream the egg yolks in the top pan (off the heat) with 2 tablespoons of sugar. Heat half the milk with the remaining sugar and the vanilla until boiling. Pour on to the yolks, stirring all the time. Put the pan over the hot water and stir gently until the custard will coat the spoon (about 15 minutes). Add the remaining milk and leave until cold, stirring occasionally.

Add the whisky and finely chopped praline and fold in the whisked cream. Freeze in an ice cream maker, or in the freezer, beating after 2 hours. Smooth the ice cream into the same tin that was used for baking the cake and freeze for 2 hours.

Cut the sponge horizontally into 3 (freeze the other layers to use on another occasion). Cover the golden vanilla ice with a layer of cake, sprinkle it well with 4 tablespoons of whisky, and return to the freezer.

LANDSCAPE IN NORTHERN SPAIN *The greener areas of northern Spain are a source of the dairy produce, particularly milk and cream, which figures in many desserts.*

For the white ice cream, whisk the egg whites to soft peaks then sprinkle with 125 g (4 oz) of sugar. Whisk this for 2–3 minutes, until the mixture has the gloss of high-quality satin. With the same beaters whisk the cream, adding the vanilla. Fold the meringue and cream together, cutting down with the edge of a big metal spoon 6–7 times. Remove the cake tin from the freezer and spoon the ice cream over the cake layer, smoothing the top. Slide the caramel disc on top, pressing it on very gently, and freeze overnight.

Carefully remove the cake tin from round the cake and use a palette knife to scoop up the coarsely chopped praline, pressing it into the side of the cake. Slide it on to a serving plate. Whisk the cream with 2 tablespoons of sugar and pipe rosettes on top round the edge, one on each portion. Dust each one with the last crumbs left from the praline. Return to the freezer until needed: a convenient party cake, it is soft enough to serve without defrosting. A sparkling Cava wine from Codorníu is just the thing to accompany it.

ROSCÓN DE REYES

TWELFTH NIGHT YEAST CAKE

Christmas presents come on Twelfth Night, January 6th, in Spain and it is not Father Christmas who brings them, but *Los Reyes Magos*, the three wise men, who arrived bearing gifts for Christ. This ornamental ring bread, eaten at tea-time, has a little surprise hidden in it, formerly a single bean, similar to Provençal Twelfth Night cake.

Mesonero Romanos describes the scene as it used to be in *Un año en Madrid* published in 1852. The cake is cut into equal slices and covered with a napkin 'to avoid favouritism or cheats'. Everyone is then given a slice, to the accompaniment of traditional songs. Whoever gets the *haba* or surprise is declared King of the festival and is in charge of entertainments during the evening. The King's last duty is to invite everyone to a feast on the following Sunday, at which he relinquishes his kingship. The author laments that the custom has disappeared in Madrid (perhaps wives objected to this extra post-Christmas entertaining) and that the latter feast has become a breakfast or *merienda* – afternoon snack.

The festive bread in the picture was made with double the amount of dough. However it was very difficult to handle and the recipe below, slightly adapted from Janet Mendel Searl's lovely book *Cooking in Spain*, is easier, though a food processor should not be used to knead the dough.

SERVES 10 – 12

250 g (9 oz) strong plain flour
½ teaspoon salt
15 g (½ oz) dried yeast
6 tablespoons milk, warmed
50 g (2 oz) sugar
50 g (2 oz) butter, softened
2 medium-sized eggs (size 3)
1 egg white, lightly beaten
2 teaspoons dark rum
2 teaspoons orange flower water
1 teaspoon finely grated orange zest
1 teaspoon finely grated lemon zest
25 g (1 oz) almond flakes
candied fruit, including cherries, for decoration

Make a starter dough. Mix the yeast with 1 teaspoon of sugar and the milk (at blood temperature). Stir in 50 g (2 oz) flour to make a wet paste. Stand in a warm place – a gas oven with a pilot light, or the oven at its lowest setting 40° C (100° F) – for 20 30 minutes, until it is very frothy.

Meanwhile sift the remaining flour with the salt into a large bowl and stir in the rest of the sugar and the orange and lemon zests. Rub in the butter until the mixture resembles fine breadcrumbs.

Beat the eggs with the rum and orange flower water. Make a well in the middle of the flour and add the eggs and the yeast starter. Use a wooden spoon to mix to a sticky dough. Then use one hand to slap the mixture backwards and forwards until it loses its stickiness. Be patient – even working vigorously the process will take at least 10 minutes, and is not successful in a food processor, where it becomes even stickier.

Transfer the dough to a lightly floured surface and continue slapping and kneading for a further 5–10 minutes, until it is very smooth and elastic. Put the dough in a clean, oiled bowl, cover with a tea towel and leave in a warm place for 1 hour until doubled in bulk.

Punch the dough down on a lightly floured surface to its original size. Slip in the *haba*, generally a little china rabbit or figure, or a coin, then shape the dough into a sausage that will fit snugly into a greased, push-bottom 22 cm (9 in) ring tin. Cover again and put in a warm place for 45 minutes to rise once more.

Heat the oven to 180° C (350° F, gas 4). Brush the top with lightly beaten egg white and sprinkle with almonds and candied fruit. Bake for 30 minutes, until risen and golden brown. Let it stand for 5 minutes, then push out of the tin and let it cool on a wire rack.

ROSCÓN DE REYES

ENSAIMADA

MALLORCAN SWEET BREAD ROLLS

Half way between a bun and pastry, these delicious sweet rolls are sent regularly from Mallorca to Barcelona, where they are a popular choice for breakfast. Their spiral shape is often compared to an Arab's turban, but I think it has a far older, and more feminine, origin in the *cabessal*. This is the spiral of twisted strips of cloth that is placed on a woman's head to enable her to balance a pitcher of water or basket. In Europe it dates back at least to classical times, and only died out in nearby Languedoc in the 19th century. Larger *ensaimadas* are still made – the size of 'basket bottoms' – and are sometimes decorated with a slice of the local *sobrasada* sausage.

Saim means 'lard', which is traditional, but butter has replaced it, and it is used to separate the rings of bread as they expand. The recipe is a way of experiencing the old-fashioned pleasure that comes from handling bread dough.

MAKES 10 ROLLS

300 g (10 oz) strong plain flour
½ teaspoon salt
½ of 15 g sachet or 1½ teaspoons dried yeast
125 ml (4 fl oz) milk, warm
4 tablespoons sugar
3 tablespoons sunflower oil, plus extra for greasing
1 large egg
2 tablespoons butter, melted
1 tablespoon honey
icing sugar, for sifting

Make a starter dough with the yeast. Put it in a bowl with 1 tablespoon of sugar and the milk (at a temperature that feels neither hot nor cold to your finger). Stir in 75 g (3 oz) of flour to make a smooth sticky cream. Put this in a warm place, such as in a gas oven with a pilot light, or the oven on lowest setting (40° C, [100° F]), until it is very frothy and doubled in size, about 20 minutes.

Meanwhile, put the remaining flour, salt and sugar into a food processor. Or sieve the flour with the salt into a large bowl and stir in the rest of the sugar. Beat the egg with the oil. Add the egg mixture and the frothy starter dough to the processor, or to a well in the middle of the dry ingredients. Process to a smooth elastic dough. Alternatively, use a wooden spoon to stir the two together, pulling the flour into the liquid. When a stiffish paste forms, switch to working with one hand. Knead the crumbs into the dough until it is a soft but not sticky ball. Flour a working surface lightly and knead the dough by pulling and stretching it, then slapping together again, until it is elastic and smooth.

Pull off egg-sized lumps of dough, about 50 g (2 oz), and roll each one out. With 8 fingers spread, roll it to and fro, moving the fingers outwards until the roll is nearly as slim as a pencil, but twice the length. (The old way was to do this with hands coated in butter.) Pour the melted butter on to a plate and pass each roll through it, holding on to the ends. Tuck one end in and roll the sausage into a spiral, down on to a lightly greased baking sheet, then tuck the free end under so it can't come adrift. Leave plenty of room between the rolls. Cover the tray with a tea towel and leave in a warm place for about 1 hour, until the rolls have doubled in size.

Heat the oven to 190° C (375° F, gas 5). Dissolve the honey with 1 tablespoon of hot water, then brush the rolls once. Bake for 12 minutes, until pale golden brown. Remove them to a wire rack to cool, and brush them again with the honey mixture. Leave to cool for 5 minutes, then dust with icing sugar. Serve warm.

BRAZO GITANO

'GIPSY'S ARM' ROLLED SPONGE CAKE

The brown arms of the gipsy, perhaps raised with castanets in hand, provide the visual image behind the name of this long, thin sponge roll, with its filling of chocolate, flavoured with cinnamon and rum.

SERVES 6 – 8

SPONGE
5 large eggs
100 g (3½ oz) caster sugar, plus extra for sprinkling
4 tablespoons plain flour
pinch of salt
finely grated zest of 1 lemon
butter for greasing

CREMA PASTELERA AL RON
300 ml (½ pt) milk, hot
100 g (4 oz) dark chocolate, broken into small pieces
3 large egg yolks
100 g (3½ oz) sugar
1 tablespoon flour
2 tablespoons cornflour
¼ teaspoon powdered cinnamon
4 tablespoons rum
½ teaspoon vanilla extract

Heat the oven to 180° C (350° F, gas 4) and line a Swiss roll tray 45 × 26 cm (15 × 10½ in) with non-stick baking paper. Grease it well with butter. Separate the eggs which should be at room temperature. Since most Spanish kitchens have temperatures in the 30s Centigrade (80s Fahrenheit), I stand the bowl with the yolks inside a saucepan of hot tap water: this works very well. Grate the lemon zest on your finest grater, using a little of the measured sugar to mop up the oil. Add the zest and about half the sugar to the yolks. Whisk hard until they look like a thick pale custard – 2 – 3 minutes.

Whisk the whites with the salt until soft peaks form. Gradually add the remaining sugar and whisk to a glossy meringue. Fold the meringue into the egg yolks, cutting down with the side of a large metal spoon. Sift the flour over the top, a little at a time, and fold in.

Pour into the prepared tray and bake for 12 – 15

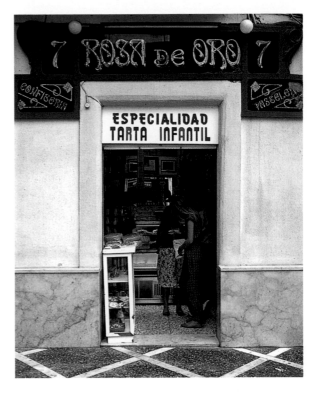

CAKE SHOP *In addition to their everyday fare, cake shops offer unique sweets for special feast days, made only at that time of year.*

minutes until pale brown and springy to the touch.

Have a sheet of non-stick baking paper prepared and sprinkled with caster sugar. Turn the cake out on to the sugared paper and remove the lining paper. Trim off the crisp edges and roll up from one of the long sides, with the sugared paper inside. Wrap it in a dampened tea towel, well wrung out, and leave until cold.

Make the filling. Melt the chocolate in a bowl over simmering water, stirring occasionally. Stir the egg yolks, flour, cornflour and cinnamon together to make a paste, adding a little milk if needed. Bring the milk and sugar to boiling point then pour on to the yolks, stirring. Return to the pan. Cook over low heat, stirring continuously, as the mixture is lumpy at first, until the custard is very thick and smooth. Off the heat, stir in the melted chocolate, vanilla and rum. Cover the surface of the custard with a piece of cling film to prevent a skin forming and leave until cold.

Unwrap the sponge, spread with chocolate filling and re-roll. Wrap the paper round it until needed. Chill and serve the same day.

PASTEL VASCO

BASQUE CHERRY TART

This is the world's greatest picnic tart, for the heavy sweet pastry that the Spaniards love so well is perfect for eating outdoors. It has the texture and taste of sponge cake and is frequently cooked with a thick layer of custard in the middle. The earliest version of this tart was probably bread dough with a wild cherry jam inside, and cooked Morello cherries make the most delicious centre. You can also use fresh black cherries, if these are available.

SERVES 6

215 g (7½ oz) flour, sifted, plus extra for rolling
1 teaspoon baking powder
pinch of salt
100 g (4 oz) cold unsalted butter, diced
75 g (3 oz) caster sugar, plus extra for sprinkling
2 small eggs (size 4)
grated zest of ½ lemon
700 g (1½ lb) bottled or cooked Morello cherries in syrup, or 2 cans (400 g [14 oz] size) cherries, or 500 g (1 lb) fresh black cherries

Put the flour, baking powder and salt into a food processor and work in the butter, or rub it in with your fingers to make coarse crumbs. Add the lemon zest, using a little of the measured sugar to pick up the lemon oil from the grater. Work in all the sugar, 1 whole egg and the yolk of the second, to make a soft dough. Divide the dough into 2, one portion nearly twice the size of the other, and pat into 2 flat cakes. Put the dough cakes on plates and chill for at least 2 hours, preferably longer.

Heat the oven to 170°C (325°F, gas 3) with a baking sheet in it. Grease a 20 cm (8 in) loose-bottomed sponge-sandwich tin or a flan tin. Leave the smaller piece of pastry in the refrigerator and roll out the larger portion on a floured work surface to 2.5 cm (1 in) larger all round than the tin. Fold the pastry edges inwards all round and slide the loose tin bottom under the pastry to pick it up. Put into position in the tin. This is a 'press-in' pastry, so fit it evenly round the sides, without any trimming, so that it stands just clear of the top.

Stone the cherries, draining them in a sieve, then blot well on kitchen paper. Distribute the cherries in the pastry case, packing them in tightly. Roll out the pastry lid to fit inside the ring and position it on top. Fold the edge of the pastry case inwards over the lid and press gently all round with a fork, just pulling the pastry away from the sides of the tin at the top.

Prick the lid in a few places, brush with the remaining egg white and sprinkle with a little sugar. Bake on the hot sheet for 45–55 minutes until golden. Let the tart stand for 5 minutes, then push upwards out of the ring, and remove from the base. Let it cool on a wire rack.

MANTECADOS

CINNAMON SAND CAKES

Made all over Spain, these little dry biscuits are closely related to *polvorones*, 'crumble cakes'. They combine flour, sugar and eggs, with an infinity of small local variations. In one town they might include a little ground almond, in another a glass of anis or the colourless *eau-de-vie, aguardiente. Mantecado* actually means 'lardy cake', though they are more often made with butter nowadays. They are eaten for their texture, as a partner to dessert wine or ice cream, and almost never by themselves.

MAKES 12—15

250 g (½ lb) flour
75 g (3 oz) blanched almonds
150 g (5 oz) unsalted butter, diced
150 g (5 oz) caster sugar
½ teaspoon ground cinnamon

Heat the oven to 180° C (350° F, gas 4). Spread out the flour on a baking tray and toast until lightly coloured – about 8 – 10 minutes. Toast the almonds in the oven for rather longer, until lightly biscuit-coloured, then grind to a powder in a blender. Turn the oven down to 130° C (250° F, gas ½).

Beat the butter with the sugar and cinnamon until creamy, then mix in the flour and almonds. Turn the dough on to a work surface – it is incredibly crumbly.

Pat into a mass about 1.5 cm (½ in) thick, then cut out with an upturned sherry glass or a plain 5 cm (2 in) biscuit cutter. Move them on a palette knife to a greased baking tray and bake for 30 minutes. Move carefully after baking, as they are very fragile. In Spain they are often wrapped.

Put a bowl of tangerines on the table and partner them with a glass of Scholtz Hermanos Solera 1885. A widely distributed Malaga dessert wine, this has a smell of walnuts about it, as well as the usual sultanas. It is nevertheless not a wine to drink with puddings, because of its bitter-sweet edge.

ALMOND ORCHARD *Almonds were introduced by the Moors and remain an essential ingredient of many desserts.*

DESSERTS AND DRINKS

ALFAJORES

ARAB ALMOND SWEETMEATS

Medina Sidonia is a hill town with an astonishing view of Cadiz harbour in the distance, from which the commander of the Armada must once have watched Drake 'singe the King of Spain's beard'. Below the castle, in the town square, is a small shop selling an amazing assortment of traditional sweetmeats.

According to the Spanish epicure, Luis Antonio de Vega in *Viaje por La Cocina Española*, Medina Sidonia was 'once the sweetmeat capital of the Muslim world ... In the 11th century the town exported cooks for the *seraglios* of the most opulent Muslim lords of Asia and Africa, some of whom, because they were women of great beauty, became the mothers of caliphs, kings and viziers – aided a little by the scents of their cooking pots'. Naturally enough, the recipes are secret, but this is very close.

Honey and almonds are a favourite Arab combination and Spain specializes in single-flower honeys, like orange flower. *Alfajores* make good Christmas sweets rolled in coloured papers, like *amaretti*.

MAKES 14–15

100 g (4 oz) almonds, including some unblanched ones
200 g (7 oz) sealed packet of ground almonds
2 tablespoons currants
½ teaspoon aniseed, roughly crushed
grated zest of ½ lemon
1 teaspoon ground cinnamon
200 g (7 oz) thick honey
icing sugar for coating

Toast the whole almonds in a low oven (about 150° C (300° F, gas 2) shaking the pan occasionally, until they are biscuit-coloured and give off a pleasant smell (about 20 minutes), then chop coarsely. Snip the currants up in a cup with scissors, until very small.

Put the ground almonds, cinnamon, currants and aniseed into a bowl, adding the grated lemon zest, using a little of the ground almond to pick up the lemon oil off the grater. Warm the honey and stir into the mixture with a stout spoon. Add the chopped almonds and knead them in well with your hands.

Before the mixture gets cold, pull off bits and roll them in a tray of icing sugar to make small bullet shapes. Wrap each one in a square of coloured tissue, twisting both ends. Black coffee and an orange liqueur like Triple Sec make a natural accompaniment.

MELOCOTÓN ASADO EN VINO TINTO

PEACHES BAKED IN RED WINE

Pears baked in red wine with cinnamon are well known: less well known is that they come from Galicia. Peaches in red wine are less familiar, and I first ate them in a monastery in Navarre, high in the foothills of the Pyrenees. Spanish table wines are cheap, fruity and uncomplicated – ideal for cooking. I look for Navarra wine, but it hardly matters.

Soft vanilla ice cream is the perfect partner: try the white ice cream on page 128, which takes two minutes to make and needs no beating.

SERVES 6

6 large peaches
50 g (2 oz) caster sugar, plus 3 tablespoons
500 ml (18 fl oz) red wine, preferably Navarra

Heat the oven to 180° C (350° F, gas 4). Choose a suitable container for baking the peaches, one in which they will fit tightly. Dip each peach in boiling water for 10 seconds, then skin them and arrange in the baking dish.

Heat half the wine with 50 g (2 oz) sugar, stirring to dissolve it. Add the remaining wine, bring to a simmer, then pour over the peaches. Bake, covered with foil, for 30 minutes, basting once and spinning the peaches if they are not submerged. Sprinkle the tops with sugar and move to the top shelf, if your oven has the element at the top. Alternatively, slip under a hot grill for 2–3 minutes. Cool in the wine, then chill. Serve on glass dishes with a little pool of red wine on each one.

HORSE AND CART IN ARAGON *A traditional form of transport is used to carry the shopping home.*

136

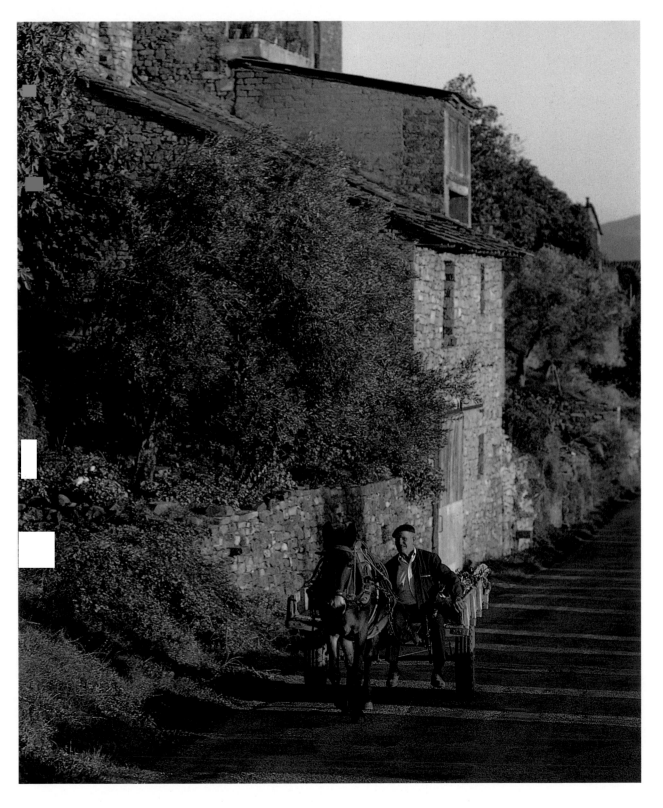

FRESAS CON ANIS

STRAWBERRIES WITH ANIS

Strawberries are ripe just in time for Easter in Spain and some of the most luscious berries are grown round Aranjuez, where the Kings of Spain have the most beautiful summer palace. Chinchón, where one of the best brands of anis is made, is just a few kilometres away and anis makes the ideal dressing for them. In the south, a medium sweet *oloroso* sherry is used for the same purpose: cream is much less common.

SERVES 4

500 g (1 lb) strawberries
4 tablespoons anis
2 tablespoons caster sugar

Sprinkle the hulled berries with anis and sugar and leave for 'the time it takes to dance a *sardana*' – about 30 minutes. If the weather is very hot, serve on a glass plate, standing it in a shallow bowl of crushed ice.

EMPANADILLAS DE CIDRA

SWEET DEEP-FRIED PASTRIES

Frying-pan sweets, *dulces de sartén*, are common in Andalusia, the best-known being the *churro* rings that are made before your eyes in every market. The reason for frying them is simple. Houses traditionally have no ovens – it is simply too hot to use them so far south.

Empanadillas, which means 'little pies', are the only sweet food sold in *tapas* bars. They usually have a shell marking on the outside, so may well be turned out by some sort of waffle iron. These home-made ones are smaller and are quite irresistible when newly made, so I have allowed 4 or 5 to a portion.

In the centre of each one is Spain's favourite jam, called 'angel's hair', *cabello de ángel*. It is made from *cidra*, an oval, melon-like squash, dark green but mottled yellow, which has very stringy flesh. Often the jam filling is omitted and sesame seeds included in the dough instead. In this case they are called *borrachuelos*, 'drunken doughnuts', because they are then well dunked in the syrup.

SERVES 4

175 g (6 oz) flour, plus extra for rolling
¼ teaspoon salt
2 tablespoons sunflower oil
25 g (1 oz) unsalted butter
100 ml (3½ fl oz) white wine, not too dry
thinly pared zest of 1 lemon
½ teaspoon aniseeds, crushed (optional)
100 g (4 oz) 'angel's hair', or another stiff jam
100 g (4 oz) thick honey
2 tablespoons brandy
caster sugar for coating
olive oil for deep frying

Heat the oil with lemon zest until it browns, then discard the zest. Add the butter, wine and aniseed, if using, and stir together. Remove from the heat and beat in the flour, with the salt, a little at a time until it forms a smooth dough. Remove from the pan and knead the dough briefly. Then let it rest in a plastic bag in the refrigerator for 2 hours.

Roll out the dough as thinly as you can on a floured surface. Traditionally it is then cut with a wine glass into 6 cm (2½ in) circles. Spoon about ½ teaspoon of jam on one half, with your finger dampen all round the edge with water, and fold them in half. Seal the edges by pressing with a fork.

Heat fresh oil for deep frying. Make a syrup for dipping the doughnuts by melting the honey and brandy together. When a bread cube will crisp in about 40 seconds (top setting on an electric fryer), fry the pies, 4 or 5 at a time. They will usually bob to the surface when they start to expand. Spin them over with a slotted spoon and fry until golden. Drain on kitchen paper, while you fry the next batch.

Dip the *empanadillas* into the syrup and place them on a wire rack. When they are all ready, transfer to a plate and sprinkle with sugar. Eat within half a day – if they last so long.

SANGRÍA

CHILLED WINE
AND CITRUS FRUIT PUNCH

At 4 o'clock on a hot summer afternoon, when the late lunch time customary in Spain is approaching, a jug of iced red wine and citrus fruit punch is the most welcome thing in the world.

SERVES 4

1 bottle red wine, chilled
juice of 4 oranges
juice of 2 lemons, plus 2 strips of zest
2 tablespoons caster sugar
750 ml (1¼ pt) soda water, chilled
6–8 ice cubes

Pour the wine over the ice cubes in a large bowl and add the strips of lemon zest. Squeeze the fruit juices, stir in the sugar and make up to 1½ l (2½ pt) with soda water. Add this to the wine and serve in a large jug, glass or Spanish earthenware. Many Spanish shops will sell you one painted in blue with '*sangría*' on it.

EL CARAJILLO

BRANDIED COFFEE

The *guardia civil* no longer wear the shiny black patent leather hat, squashed at the back, that they did in Franco's time. But in country districts they still patrol in pairs on motor bikes – chilly work in the mountains that make up so much of Spain. You can see them in bars, where so many people breakfast, having their morning drink of coffee and brandy before they set off.

SERVES 2

strong black coffee for 2
2 tablespoons Spanish brandy
sugar (for those that like it)

Make a good cup of coffee, *demi-tasse* size, and add a tablespoon of brandy. Anis de Chinchón makes a very good alternative to brandy.

FARMHOUSE *A vine trained over the farmhouse wall provides fresh grapes for the inhabitants.*

INDEX

A

acelgas see chard
acelgas con pasas y piñones   65
aguardiente   10
ajo blanco con uvas de Málaga   32
alcachofas see artichokes
alcachofas con dos salsas   74
alfajores   136
alioli: egg yolk alioli   54
    fragrant rice followed by fish and
        alioli   54–5
    roast leg of lamb with quince alioli
        101
almendras see almonds
almonds   10
    Arab almond sweetmeats   136
    chicken fricassee with almond sauce
        111
    chilled almond soup, Malaga-style,
        with grapes   32
    cinnamon sand cakes   134–5
    praline   128
    mountain trout with piquant almond
        sauce   88
alpargatas valencianas   106
alubias see beans
amanida catalana   77
anchovies: baked aubergine and red
        pepper salad with   75
    effortless anchovy salad   24
angulas   20
anis, strawberries with,   138
apples: monkfish in apple and cider
        sauce   86
Arabs *see* Moors
Arab almond sweetmeats   136
arroz a banda   54–5
arroz con costra al estilo de Elche   56
arroz con jerez   58
artichokes   10
    artichokes with two sauces   74
    cooking whole   74
    preparing bases   103
    veal with artichokes from Cordoba
        103
asparagus: scrambled eggs with young
        asparagus   45
Asturian bean and sausage pot   106–7
aubergines: baked aubergine and red
        pepper salad with anchovies   75
avellanas see hazelnuts
azafrán see saffron

B

bacalao see salt cod

bacalao en samfaina   88–9
barbecue   42, 65, 82, 88, 100
Basque cherry tart   134
Basque pepper omelette   45
beans   10, 42, 62, 72
    Asturian bean and sausage pot 106–7
    Galician cabbage soup   38
    Uncle Luke's mildly spiced
        beans   70
beef   100
    stew with chestnuts and
        pears   102–3
    steak, with baked aubergines and
        pepper salad   75
Bilbao mixed vegetable pot   67
biscuits   124
    cinnamon sand cakes   134–5
blue cheese sauce, roast venison with
    119
boquerones sin trabajo   24
brandy   10
    brandied coffee   139
brazo gitano   133
bread   10
    Mallorcan sweet bread rolls   132
    tomato bread with raw ham and
        cheese   28
    Twelfth Night yeast cake   130
breadcrumbs, crisp fried   70
broad beans with ham, Ronda style   66
buñuelos   124
    buñuelos de queso   24
burnt Catalan cream   125
butifarra   10
butter   12
butter beans: Asturian bean and sausage
    pot   106–7

C

cabbage   62
    cabbage soup, Galician   38
Cabrales cheese   11
Cadiz fish soup with orange   38
cakes: 'gipsy's arm' rolled sponge cake
    133
calçots amb romesco   65
caldillo de perro   38
caldo gallego   38
canelones con langostinos   59
canela see cinnamon
cannelloni   42
    fried cannelloni with prawns   59
carabineros con whisky   85
el carajillo   139
caramel: burnt Catalan cream   125
    orange caramel creams   127
    orange ice cream with brittle

caramel   128
cardo see cardoon
cardoon   11, 62
carne con castañas y peras   102–3
Catalan arranged salad   77
Catalan salt cod and pepper salad   83
cauliflower, fried   63
cayenne pepper   14
cebollas see onions
champiñones rellenos   23
chanquetes   27
chard   11
    spinach with raisins and pine-nuts 65
cheese   11
    hot fried cheese puffs   24
    roast venison with blue cheese sauce
        119
    tomato bread with raw ham and
        cheese   28
cherry tart, Basque   134
chestnuts: beef with chestnuts and
        pears   102–3
chicken: boneless garlic chicken
        morsels   22
    chicken fricassee with almond
        sauce   111
    chicken with red pepper, ham and
        tomatoes   110
    hare, chicken, ham and liver terrine
        120–1
    rice with chicken and seafood   53
    roast, with *romesco* sauce   88
chickpeas   11, 62
    chickpea and sausage stew   72
chillies   11, 88
    sizzling chilli-hot prawns   27
chocolate   124
    'gipsy's arm' rolled sponge
        cake   133
    partridge with chocolate sauce
        114–15
    Valencia chocolate mousse   125
chorizo   11–12
    stuffed mushrooms   23
cider   12
    monkfish in apple and cider sauce 86
cinnamon   12
    beef with chestnuts and
        pears   102–3
    cinnamon sand cakes   134–5
    little meat espadrilles in wine sauce
        106
clams   82
    clam sauce, poached eggs with   51
cocido   20, 37, 100
    cocido Madrileño   104–5
cod *see* salt cod

codornices asadas con ajos 117
coffee, brandied 139
coliflor al estilo de Badajoz 63
conejo guisado a la burgalesa 118–19
cordero asado con alioli de membrillo 101
cordero en ajillo pastor 102
cream 124
crema catalana 125
custards: burnt Catalan cream 125
    orange caramel creams 127
cuttlefish 16, 82
    cleaning 95
    cuttlefish with peas and
        meatballs 95

D
desserts 123–38
drinks 124, 139
duck, roast duck with dried figs 116–17

E
eels 20, 42
eggs 42
    Basque pepper omelette 45
    clear soup with ham, egg and
        mint 35
    colourful baked eggs 46
    fragrant rice followed by fish and
        alioli 54–5
    garlic soup with poached eggs 35
    pepper salad with tuna and egg 78
    poached eggs with clam sauce 51
    rice with a crisp egg crust 56
    scrambled eggs with wild
        mushrooms 46
    scrambled eggs with young
        asparagus 45
    Spanish potato omelette 43
    tomato stew with deep-fried
        eggs 50
empanada de raxó 108
empanadillas de cidra 138
ensaimada 132
ensalada de naranjas valencianas 74–5
ensaladilla 78–9
escabeche de perdices 118
escalivada con anchoas 75
esqueixada 83

F
fabada asturiana 106–7
fat 12
fideuà de mariscos 58–9
figs: roast duck with dried
        figs 116–17
fish 81–94
    fragrant rice followed by fish and

alioli 54–5
    medley of fish 94
    mixed fried fish, Malaga style 85
    stock 16, 54, 59
    see also monkfish, salt cod *etc.*
flan 124
    flan de naranja 127
fresas con anis 138
fricassee: chicken fricassee with almond
        sauce 111
fritos de pescado a la Malagueña 85
fruit 124
    fruit butter, alioli 101

G
Galician cabbage soup 38
Galician pork and sausage pie 108
gambas en gabardinas 26
gambas pil-pil 27
garbanzos see chickpeas
garbanzos y chorizos 72
garlic 12
    boneless garlic chicken morsels 22
    garlic soup with poached eggs 35
    roast leg of lamb with quince alioli
        101
    roast quail with garlic cloves 117
    wild mushrooms with garlic 66
gazpacho rojo de Sevilla 32
'gipsy's arm' rolled sponge cake 133
grapes: chilled almond soup,
        Malaga-style, with grapes 32
green beans:
    Bilbao mixed vegetable pot 67
guinea fowl, roast 117

H
habas Rondeñas 66
haddock: in cider sauce 86
hake: Cadiz fish soup with orange 38
    hake with green sauce 83
ham 12–13
    broad beans with ham, Ronda style
        66
    chicken with red pepper, ham and
        tomatoes 110
    clear soup with ham, egg and
        mint 35
    hare, chicken, ham and liver
        terrine 120–1
    little meat espadrilles in wine
        sauce 106
    tomato bread with raw ham and
        cheese 28
hare, chicken, ham and liver
        terrine 120–1
haricot beans: Uncle Luke's mildly

spiced beans 68
hazelnuts 10
    frozen whisky layer cake 128–9
huevos escalfados con almejas 49
huevos a la flamenca 46

I
ice creams 124
    frozen whisky layer cake 128–9
    orange ice cream with brittle
        caramel 128
ingredients 10–17

J
jamón serrano 13
    with broad beans 66
    soup with egg, mint and 35
judías blancas a lo Tío Lucas 68

K
kebabs, small spicy Moorish 21
kidneys: tartlets of kidneys in
        sherry 23

L
lamb 100
    roast leg of lamb with quince
        alioli 101
    shepherd's aromatic lamb stew 102
leek and potato soup 37
liver: hare, chicken, ham and liver
        terrine 120–1
lomo embuchado 13
longaniza 13

M
mackerel and red pepper stew 87
Madrid boiled meat dinner 104–5
Mallorcan sweet bread rolls 132
Manchego cheese 11
manteca colorada 28
mantecados 134–5
marmitako 87
marquesa de chocolate valenciana 125
mayonnaise: cold monkfish in
        mayonnaise with rice salad 90
    'little' or 'Russian' salad 78–9
meat 99–121
    cured meats 12, 100
    Madrid boiled meat dinner 104–5
    see also beef, chicken *etc.*
meatballs: cuttlefish with peas and
        meatballs 95
    meat balls in red sherry sauce 21
mejillones a la marinera 96
mejillones con pimiento verde y rojo 26–7
melocotón asado en vino tinto 136

menestra a la Bilbaina 67
merluza con salsa verde 83
migas de pastor 70
monkfish: cold monkfish in mayonnaise
     with rice salad 90
   monkfish in apple and cider
        sauce 86
Moors 10, 13–15, 21, 42, 62, 111, 124,
     136
morcilla 13
morteruelo 120–1
mountain trout with piquant almond
        sauce 88
mousse, Valencia chocolate 125
mushrooms 13, 66
   scrambled eggs with wild
        mushrooms 46
   stuffed mushrooms 23
   wild mushrooms with garlic 66
mussels: cold stuffed mussels with
        peppers 26–7
   sailors' spicy mussels 96

O
octopus: festive spiced octopus salad 97
olive oil 12, 13
olives 20, 62
omelettes: Basque pepper omelette 45
   Spanish potato omelette 43
onions 14
   Valencian orange and onion salad
        74–5
oranges 124
   Cadiz fish soup with orange 38
   orange caramel creams 127
   orange ice cream with brittle
        caramel 128
   Valencian orange and onion salad
        74–5

P
pa amb tomàquet con jamón y queso 28
pacharán 14, 94
paella 42
   fragrant rice followed by fish and
        alioli 54–5
   paella of spring vegetables 54
   rice with chicken and seafood 53
   rice with a crisp egg crust 56
paella de verduras del tiempo 54
paella valenciana 53
paprika 14
   paprika pork rillettes 28
   spicy fried potatoes 71
partridge: partridge with chocolate
        sauce 114–15
   roast partridge 117

soused partridges 118
pasta 42
   fried cannelloni with prawns 59
   pasta with seafood 58–9
pastel vasco 134
pastries, sweet deep-fried 138
pastry: cornmeal 23
   sweet 134
   wine 108
patatas picantes 71
pato con higos 116–17
peaches baked in red wine 136
pears: beef with chestnuts and pears
     102–3
peas: cuttlefish with peas and meatballs
     95
   hake with green sauce 83
pelotas en salsa roja 21
pepitoria de gallina 111
pepper 15
peppers 14
   baked aubergine and red pepper
        salad with anchovies 75
   Basque pepper omelette 45
   Catalan salt cod and pepper
        salad 83
   chicken with red pepper, ham and
        tomatoes 110
   cold stuffed mussels with peppers
        26–7
   colourful baked eggs 46
   grilled red peppers with cream 63
   mackerel and red pepper stew 87
   peeling 63, 75
   pepper salad with tuna and egg 78
perdiz en chocolate 114–15
pie, Galician pork and sausage 108
pimientos con nata 63
pinchitos morunos 21
pine-nuts 14
   spinach with raisins and pine-nuts 65
piperrada Vasca 45
piriñaca 78
pisto manchego con huevos fritos 48
pixin a la asturiana 86
poached eggs with clam sauce 51
pollo al ajillo al estilo de parellada 22
pollo en chilindrón 110
polvorones 124, 134
pork 100
   chops, *samfaina* sauce for 88
   Galician pork and sausage pie 108
   little meat espadrilles in wine sauce
        106
   meatballs in red sherry sauce 21
   paprika pork rillettes 28
   small spicy Moorish kebabs 21

pork fat 12
potatoes 62
   leek and potato soup 37
   'little' or 'Russian' salad 78–9
   Spanish potato omelette 43
   spicy fried potatoes 71
praline: frozen whisky layer cake 128–9
prawns 82
   fried cannelloni with prawns 59
   large prawns with whisky 85
   prawns 'in mackintoshes' 26
   sizzling chilli-hot prawns 27
pulpo a la feria 97
punch: chilled wine and citrus fruit
        punch 139
purrusalda 37

Q
quail: roast quail with garlic
        cloves 117
queimada 124
quinces: roast leg of lamb with quince
        alioli 101

R
rabbit: stewed rabbit from
        Burgos 118–19
raisins: spinach with raisins and
        pine-nuts 65
rape con mahonesa y ensalada de arroz 90
revuelto con setas 46
revuelto de espárragos trigueros 45
rice 14–15, 42
   cold monkfish in mayonnaise with
        rice salad 90
   fragrant rice followed by fish and
        alioli 54–5
   paella of spring vegetables 54
   rice with chicken and seafood 53
   rice with a crisp egg crust 56
   rice with sherry 58
rillettes, paprika pork 28
romesco sauce: grilled spring onions with
        romesco sauce 65
   mountain trout with piquant almond
        sauce 88
roscón de reyes 131
rovellons al ajillo 66
'Russian' salad 78–9

S
saffron 15
sailors' spicy mussels 96
St James' baked scallops 91
salads 62
   baked aubergine and red pepper
        salad with anchovies 75

Catalan arranged salad   77
Catalan salt cod and pepper
        salad   83
cold monkfish in mayonnaise with
        rice salad   90
effortless anchovy salad   24
festive spiced octopus salad   97
'little' or 'Russian' salad   78–9
pepper salad with tuna and egg   78
Valencian orange and onion
        salad   74–5
salchichón   15
salmon   82
salsa roja   21
salt   15
salt cod (*bacalao*)   10
        Catalan salt cod and pepper
                salad   83
        salt cod in mixed vegetable
                sauce   88–9
samfaina   88
sand cakes, cinnamon   134–5
sangría   139
sardines   24, 27, 82
sauces: almond   88, 111
        apple and cider   86
        blue cheese   119
        chocolate   114–15
        clam   51
        green   83
        mixed vegetable   88–9
        red sherry   21
        romesco   65, 88
        wine   106
sausage: Asturian bean and sausage
                pot   106–7
        butifarra   10
        chickpea and sausage stew   72
        chorizo   11–12
        Galician pork and sausage pie   108
        lomo embuchado   13
        longaniza   13
        morcilla   13
        salchichón   15
        sobrasada   16
scallops: cleaning   91
        St James' baked   91
seafood   81–97
        pasta with seafood   58–9
        rice with chicken and seafood   53
sepia guisada con albóndigas y guisantes   95
setas   13, 66
Sevillian chilled red soup   32
shepherd's aromatic lamb stew   102
sherry   15–16
        meatballs in red sherry sauce   21

rice with sherry   58
tartlets of kidneys in sherry   23
veal with artichokes from
        Cordoba   103
sobrasada   16
sopa de ajo con huevos   35
sopa de picadillo   35
soups   20
        Cadiz fish soup with orange   38
        chilled almond soup, Malaga-style,
                with grapes   32
        clear soup with ham, egg and
                mint   35
        Galician cabbage soup   38
        garlic soup with poached eggs   35
        leek and potato soup   37
        Sevillian chilled red soup   32
spaghetti: pasta with seafood   58–9
Spanish potato omelette   43
spinach with raisins and pine-nuts   65
spring onions: grilled spring onions
                with *romesco* sauce   65
squid   16, 20, 82, 95
        cleaning   95
stews   100
        Asturian bean and sausage
                pot   106–7
        beef with chestnuts and
                pears   102–3
        chickpea and sausage stew   72
        mackerel and red pepper stew   87
        shepherd's aromatic lamb stew   102
        stewed rabbit from Burgos   118–19
stock   16, 54, 59
strawberries with anis   138
sweet deep-fried pastries   138
sweets   123–38

T
tapas   19–28
tart, Basque cherry   134
tarta al whisky   128–9
tarta quemada helada   128
tartaletas de riñones al Jerez   23
tartlets of kidneys in sherry   23
ternera con alcachofas a la Cordobesa   103
terrine: hare, chicken, ham and
                liver   120–1
tocino   16
tomates rellenos a la alicantina   71
tomatoes   16
        Basque pepper omelette   45
        chicken with red pepper, ham and
                tomatoes   110
        colourful baked eggs   46
        meatballs in red sherry sauce   21

sauces   16, 21, 50, 88
Sevillian chilled red soup   32
stuffed tomatoes from Alicante   71
tomato bread with raw ham and
        cheese   28
tomato stew with deep-fried
        eggs   50
tortilla española   43
tostadas   51
trout: moutain trout with piquant
        almond sauce   88
truchas con salsa romesco   88
tuna   87
        pepper salad with tuna and egg   78
turkey: prune alioli for   101
Twelfth Night yeast cake   131

U
Uncle Luke's mildly spiced beans   68

V
Valencia chocolate mousse   125
Valencian orange and onion
        salad   74–5
veal   100
        with artichokes from Cordoba   103
vegetables   61–79
        Bilbao mixed vegetable pot   67
        paella of spring vegetables   54
        see also potatoes, tomatoes *etc.*
venado asado con salsa de cabrales   119
venison: roast venison with blue cheese
        sauce 119
vieiras de Santiago   91
vinegar   16

W
whisky: frozen whisky layer
        cake   128–9
        large prawns with whisky   85
whitebait, deep-fried   27
wine   16–17
        chilled wine and citrus fruit
                punch   139
        little meat espadrilles in wine
                sauce   106
        pastry   108
        peaches baked in red wine   136

Y
yeast cake, Twelfth Night   131

Z
zarzuela   94

ACKNOWLEDGMENTS

The publisher would like to thank the following photographers and organizations for their kind permission to reproduce the photographs in this book:

3 Christian Sarramon; 6–7 Zefa Picture Library; 8 Guy Bouchet; 11–17 Retrograph Archive Collection; 22 Truchot/Explorer; 25 Truchot/Explorer; 29 Christian Sarramon; 30–31 Mike Busselle's Photo Library; 34 Pascal Hinous/Agence Top; 39 Carlos Navajas; 43 Anne Gael; 44 AGE Fotostock; 48–49 Mike Busselle's Photo Library; 50–51 Carlos Navajas; 52 Zefa Picture Library; 55 J N Reichel/Agence Top; 57 Zefa Picture Library; 64 J Ducange/Agence Top; 67 Anthony Blake Picture Library; 68–69 Mike Busselle's Photo Library; 74–75 Philippe Roy/Explorer; 79 Ted Funk/Agence Top; 86–87 Philippe Roy/Explorer; 89 Christain Sarramon; 91 Robert O'Dea; 96 John Downman/Hutchison Library; 97 Philippe Roy/Explorer; 101 Carlos Navajas; 105 Carlos Navajas; 110–111 Andrew Eames/Hutchison Library; 112–113 Mike Busselle's Photo Library; 116 Mike Busselle's Photo Library; 120–121 John Miller; 129 J Ducange/Agence Top; 133 The Anthony Blake Photo Library/Gerrit Buntrock; 135 Bernard Régent/Hutchison Library; 137 François Gohier/Explorer; 139 John Miller.

Special photography by Linda Burgess for Conran Octopus: 18–19, 33, 36–37, 40–41, 47, 60–61, 72–73, 76, 80–81, 84, 92–93, 98–99, 109, 114–115, 122–123, 126–127, 131.

Thanks to:
The Levant Trading Co., 10 Holland St., London W8 4LT
Gallery of Antique Costume and Textiles, 2 Church St., London NW8

The publishers would like to thank Cambridge University Press for permission to quote from *South from Granada* by Gerald Brenan.

BIBLIOGRAPHY

Colman Andrews, *Catalan Cuisine* (has Catalan bibliography, 1988) Marina Pereyra de Azar and Nina Froud, *The Home Book of Spanish Cookery* (1974) Luis Bettonica, *Cuisine of Spain* (En. ed. 1983) George Borrow, *The Bible in Spain* (1843) Gerald Brenan, *South from Granada* (1957) Elizabeth Carter, *Majorca Food and Cookery,* (1989) Penelope Casas, *The Foods and Wines of Spain* (1985), *Tapas* (1987) Elizabeth Cass, *Spanish Cooking* (1957) Alan Davidson, *Mediterranean Seafood* (1981), *North Atlantic Seafood* (1979) Hubert Duiker, *The Wines of Rioja* (1987) Richard Ford, *Handbook for Travellers in Spain* (1845), *Gatherings from Spain* (1846) Mary Hillgarth, *Spanish Cookery* (1970) Rudolf Grewe, *The Arrival of the Tomato in Spain and Italy: Early Recipes.* Journal of Gastronomy vol 3, no 2 summer 1987, Elisabeth Luard, *The La Iña Book of Tapas* (1989) Ana MacMiadhachäin, *Spanish Regional Cookery* (1981) Charles Metcalfe and Kathryn McWhirter, *The Wines of Spain and Portugal* (1988) Barbara Norman, *The Spanish Cookbook* (1971) Elisabeth Lambert Ortiz, *The Food of Spain and Portugal* (1989) Charles Perry, *Puff Pastry is Spanish*, Petits Propos Culinaires 17 (1984) Jan Read, *The Wines of Spain* (1982), *Mitchell Beazley Pocket Guide to Spanish Wines* (1988), *Sherry and the Sherry Bodegas* (1988) Jan Read and Maïte Manjón, *Flavours of Spain* (1978), *The Wine and Food of Spain* (1987) Alicia Rios, *The Cocido Madrileño: a Case of Culinary Adhocism*, Petits Propos Culinaires 18 (1984) Janet Mendel Searl, *Cooking in Spain* (1987) Victoria Serra, *Tiá Victoria's Spanish Kitchen* (1976) María José Sevilla, *Life and Food in the Basque Country* (1989) Marimar Torres, *The Spanish Table* (1986).

Francisco Abad y Maria Rosario Ruiz, *Cocinar en Navarra* (1986) La Condesa de Pardo Bazán, *La Cocina Española Antigua* (1912) Ana Maria Calera, *Cocina Castellana* (1980), *Cocina Balear* (1983), *Cocina Valenciana* (1983), *Cocina Vasca* (1987), *Cocina Catalana* (1988), *Cocina Andaluz* (1988) Jose Carlos Capel, *Manual del Pescado* (1982) E. Thibaut Comelade, *La Cuisine Catalane* (1981) Huguette Couffignal, *La Cuisine Rustique: Pays Basque* (1971) Alvaro Cunqueiro y Araceli Filquiera Iglesias, *Cocina Gallega* (has Galician bibliography, 1988) Maïté Escurignan. *Manuel de Cuisine Basque* (1982) Manuel Arroyo González y Carlos García del Cerro, *Quesos de España* (1988) *La Mejor Cocina Extremeña Escrita por las Dos Autoras Isabel y Carmen Garcia Hernandez* (1980) Josep Lladonosa Giró, *Cocina de Ayer, Delicias de Hoy* (1984) Gourmetour, *Guia Gastronomica y Turistica de Andalucía* (1988) Angela Landa, *El Libro de la Reposteria* (1988) Elviro Martinez Y Jose Fidalgo, *Cocina Asturiana* (has Asturian bibliography 1982) Manuel Martinez Llopis, *Historia de la gastronomia española* (has bibliography of historical cookbooks, 1989) Manuel Martinez Llopis y Simone Ortega, *La Cocina Tipica de Madrid* (1987) Lourdes March, *El Libro de la Paella y de los Arroces* (1985), Ines Ortega, *El Libro de los Huevos y de las Tortillas* (1986) Dionisio Pérez, *Guía de Buen Comer Español* (1929) Enrique Sordo, *Arte Español de la Comida* (1960) José Gutiérrez Tascon, *Cocina Leonesa* (1979) Luis San Valentin, *La Cocina de Monjas* (1989) Luis Antonio de la Vega, *Viaje por la Cocina Española* (1969).